FATHERS

FATHERS

Richard Taylor

Accents Publishing • Lexington, Kentucky • 2023

Printed in the United States of America

Accents Publishing
Editor: Katerina Stoykova
Cover photo from author's personal archives

Library of Congress Control Number: 2023945797
ISBN: 978-1-961127-02-9
First Edition

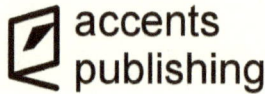

Accents Publishing is an independent press for brilliant voices. For a catalog of current and upcoming titles, please visit us on the Web at

www.accents-publishing.com

CONTENTS

For my father, Joe "Buzz" Howard Taylor,
my sons, Philip Richard Taylor and Willis Spurgin Taylor,
and my grandson, Philip Reuben Taylor

Introduction

"We are, I guess, all of us, built out of stories."
—*James Rebanks, The Shepherd's Life*

Father. The word derives from Old English *faeder* and is Germanic in origin. The Dutch is *vader*, Old Norse, *father*, the German *Vater*, all from an Indo-European root shared by Latin *Pater* and Greek *pater*. In Sanskrit the word is *pitar*. Philologists tell us that the similarities in these words unlocked the history of language. It's hard to think of a word more basic to every language unless it is *mother*. *Father* is literally seminal to human relationships and means he who begets a child, one's nearest male ancestor, or a man in relation to his children. Its metaphorical uses range from *father of his country* to its reverse in the German *fatherland* with its emphasis on the collective entity rather than the individual. *Father* was also the title by which to address a priest, a surrogate for a heavenly father—God. Working in concert with their birth partners, fathers protect, provide, nurture, and train their young. They also instruct less directly by their actions and character.

Each of us is the son or daughter of many fathers. We don't need a genealogist to tell us what we know as biological fact, though many of us might not be able to name our great grandfathers or even our grandfathers. Our bloodlines are longer than our memories, and we Americans, focused on the perfect future promised by the Age of Enlightenment, most TV commercials, and the U.S. Constitution, spend little time contemplating the past. After 8th grade biology we know that we came here from a succession of someones, progenitors named and unnamed going back to our aboriginal ancestors on the arid plains of Sub-Saharan Africa. Fathers are rooted in our culture and our understanding of ourselves as races of people. We consecrate them as patriarchs of the church. Under the English law of primogeniture, we traditionally inherited property through them, father to first son, a practice Thomas Jefferson condemned because it perpetuated an artificial aristocracy (*aristos*, the so-called "rule of the best"). We have lived until recently in what has been a largely patriarchal society, dominated by male figures, for better or for worse, often worse given our propensity to settle disputes with violence and our persistent belief that the world was made for us to rule for the benefit of our species over all others. We achieve our base identity legally and metaphorically through our parents. How many times, especially in the South, has each of us been asked, "Who is your father?" as if that told the questioner all he or she needed to know about us.

Fathers are by definition transmitters. They transmit blood and DNA, a family nose, ways of saying things, a wealth of stories, attitudes, accents of speech and ways of speaking, verbal tics and mannerisms, family lore. My father, drawing on some locution he'd doubtless grown up hearing, in moments of incredulity or frustration would exclaim, "Bush wha!" I was mystified until I finally realized what he was saying was *pshaw*, an expression of contempt or impatience, a corruption one of his parents may have misread or misheard and passed on to him.

Whether fathers transmit traits of character genetically is questionable, but for good or ill they do through their responses to the world, their outlooks and approaches to the crises that face us all. If as Wordsworth tells us, the child is father of the man, are we in part the children of our fathers and our father's fathers? Simply stated, through blood or necessary imitation, a part of our fathers lives in us and animates our thought. Fatherhood also contains the idea of succession, carried to an extreme by William Faulkner in his novel *Absalom, Absalom* in which Thomas Sutpen obsesses over producing a male heir, marrying the teenage daughter of his tenant. In my mind, *father* is as much a verb as a noun. Who fathered who, one after the other? Who fathered what? Nor does it exclude mothers, who equally influence our awakening as individuals. This collection of little essays is my unscientific attempt to offer provisional and personal answers to these questions.

In addition to our blood fathers who follow a linear progression, there are fathers as well as mothers that nourish us metaphorically through thought and imagination. Those who are not relatives also have something as intimate as blood to relate to us. My interest in the frontier and border life in the 18th century, especially in supposed heroes like Daniel Boone or Simon Kenton and so-called villains like Simon Girty or the pathologically homicidal Harpe brothers, grows from a fourth-grade Kentucky history text at Emmet Field Elementary in Louisville and to the stories of the frontier, told and retold so that my father heard or read and passed them on to me, igniting little sparks that did not fully combust for years. If fathers by definition procreate and extend the species into another generation, they also nourish and inspire the imagination, the world, real to us, we construct in our minds and that fuels our actions, as well as creativity. In my imagined world such figures as John James Audubon, Abraham Lincoln, and Cassius M. Clay are as influential as Kentucky bad boys like Simon Girty or the Civil War's Sue Mundy—male figures whose lives I have tried in words to encompass by imagining. Of course, there are also many women, the poets I most admire like Emily Dickinson or Lorine Neidecker, and recently Jane Hershfield and Mary Oliver, as well as naturalists like Lucy Braun and Mary Wharton, not to mention the leaders and innovators in our history that have left their marks on me as palpable as wrist bones or invisibly as the tattoos of memory.

Earliest surviving photo of Buzz Taylor, about 1925.

My interest in fathers began with my own father, Joe "Buzz" Howard Taylor, who has always been a mystery to me. A modest, spare-spoken man, he fathered three children, lived with one woman until his death, and led a double private life close to nature and his farming past as a relief from his public conventional life as an insurance defense lawyer. Part of that relief may have been from his family life. His heart, I am convinced, largely remained in the rural neighborhood of his youth, his life patterns at least partially formed by the stories his parents told him, their belief systems and behavior. Though he volunteered as a poll worker for every election I can remember, he was more at home with dirt under his nails, a trait he inherited from his forefathers. Both of my grandfathers died before I was born. My paternal grandfather was a relatively successful tobacco farmer who died in his early fifties of cancer when my father was a boy of twelve. My maternal grandfather, who was a supervisor of telephones and telegraphs and dispatcher for the City of Louisville, likewise died even younger, his life a cipher to me, since no one related stories about him.

What follows about my own father are the gleanings of memory, mostly fragmentary incidents that stuck with me, highlights that round out a partial portrait of a person under whose roof I lived until going off to college and even some time after. Each of us is the imperfect sum of distinguishing particulars, often traits that set one person apart from others. For example, my father entertained me as a child by demonstrating his ability to wiggle his ears. As a young man he had worked his way across the Atlantic on a cattle boat to Liverpool, England, his only trip to the land of his forefathers. He had once served the leader of America's most popular dance band, Paul Whiteman, while waiting tables in a New York City nightclub. During college he had a summer job laying cable on Pike's Peak and had once tried marijuana in the late twenties, claiming he thought nothing of it since it had no effect on him.

As a trial lawyer in a profession where dress was another form of speech, he was an indifferent dresser. He had a way of hiking his shoulders when about to speak in court as though he was afraid his shirt collar was showing. He put something on his hair and was always well combed. Unlike most lawyers, he was not a talker outside court, mostly keeping his own counsel. A man whose job required precision, he was not beyond error. Far from perfect and occasionally flummoxed, he sometimes fell victim to gaffes. Addressing a jury on his client's behalf, he was said to have once declared that the defendant had broken "all of his arms and both of his legs," an unfortunate choice of words that must have given judge and jury a laugh, and for which his partners ragged him mercilessly. Nor was he above giving questionable health tips. He enjoined me to use pine tar shampoo if I wanted to preserve a head of hair. For almost any skin ailment he prescribed witch hazel as a cure-all. In the food department, he had a penchant for such exotics as pig's feet and oxtail soup. I can remember standing in a long line with several large containers for an allotment of turtle soup cooked by a local master once a year as a fundraiser for a local church. He perfected the summertime recipe for gin and tonic, taking ritualized steps and serving them in barrel-shaped silver cups that held the ice and raised chill beads, adding a pinch of salt and squeezing his limes in an antique device I use to this day. He would not drink one from a glass. A man slightly below average in size, he was unassertive but honest to a fault, selected for years by the local Bar to serve on its ethics committee. He was not swayed by music; I never heard him sing, though he could whistle when he had a mind to, never saw him dance. With the exception of a funeral service or two, I never saw him in church, though I'm convinced that in his way he was very reverent, if not publicly pious. A big night for him was having friends over, bosom friends and their wives, to play a game called buck pitch on summer evenings on the back porch.

I can remember as a child that he cut my hair—when he noticed I was overdue for a trim, he would direct me to fetch his scissors from a drawer in my mother's dressing table—and that once I decided to save him the trouble and cut it myself. It was a botched job for which I too took a lot of ribbing. When my mother requested some wildflowers for her backyard garden, he brought home a jeepload. One of the neighbors asked him what he was doing as he transported buckets of them to a shady spot in the backyard. He allowed that he was bringing a little wildness to the domesticated precincts of Crescent Hill. Thereafter the neighbor referred to him as "Posey Toter." This did not stop the neighbor from accepting, or my father from bestowing, the bounty from his garden, distributed impartially throughout the neighborhood. Etched into my memory is the occasional live chicken he also brought home from the country, its horny legs bound with baling twine, a sock over the head. He would have me fetch his hatchet, place the bird's neck across a stump and come down hard, bringing home the expression of running about like a chicken with its head cut off. I haven't comfortably eaten chicken since.

My father was a link to another century, a living relic in some of his locutions like "much obliged," "bush wha," and "ice box." After my mother made the mistake of saying she liked cherry furniture, he also became a compulsive buyer of antiques, storing them in the attic of one of his dealer's warehouses when his own house was full. After his death, the dealer in a display of conspicuous integrity came forward and revealed the long-held secret of his cache, providing four households with fine furniture and plenty to spare. I can remember his smuggling in candlesticks under his overcoat and placing them in a bare spot in the basement that became a mound after he had filled the coal bin with his stashes. Antiques had tied him to another century he was reluctant to step out of.

"Buzz" Taylor in country garb with J.B. Myers.

His church was the primal church of nature herself. Regardless of the weather, on Sunday mornings he and his close friend, J.B. Myers (what the initials stood for I never learned) would enjoy a country breakfast together: bacon, eggs, pancakes or fried apples, sausage, grits, and black coffee. Then they would drive the back roads of eastern Jefferson County, spying out squirrels, they told me. This contest of hunter prowess must have been a throwback to their youth and that of their fathers and fathers' fathers, who as Kentuckians took pride in their marksmanship and their ability to put food on the table. Where they saw game in a mesh of trees, I saw nothing but a mass of foliage. Whether they were earnest or pulling the leg of a gullible stripling I don't know to this day, though I can attest these forays served as a kind of spiritual communion. I know too that they loved the woods that were being gnawed away for shopping malls and subdivisions and that these outings were church for them. Each Christmas they exchanged novelty gifts. In my outbuilding is a functional but utterly useless six-foot, long-handled skillet that J.B. gifted my father with red ribbon attached. My favorite photo of my father shows not the astute advocate gussied up for court and assuming a Clarence Darrow pose but the two of them standing comfortably by my father's old Willys jeep, both in khakis, a bird dog reared on J.B. Myer's chest. One knee of my father's pants is ripped out, and he's smiling, a little uncomfortable facing the camera. Both appear relaxed, amused, my camera-shy father a little perplexed, but ready. "Nimrod" was the nickname my father conferred on J.B., the mighty hunter of the Bible. Even now I like to think of the pair of them scouting in some arboreal paradise competing to count squirrels that clamber or perch half-hidden in a grove of heavenly oaks.

CRESCENT HILL: THE OLD NEIGHBORHOOD

The Crescent Hill neighborhood in which my father endured his teen years is an earlier version of the Crescent Hill I experienced, growing up in the fifties, nearly thirty years later. Names of the businesses changed, the interurban cars were replaced by freight trains throwing sooty clouds along the corridor of rails that split the area into southern and northern, but the essential character of the neighborhood remained—vertical middle-class homes along tree-lined streets. The bulbous water tower of the Louisville Water Works that dominated the skyline for blocks has come down, but many of the old landmarks remain. A visitor familiar with the area forty years ago would not be shaken by a radical transformation.

Somewhere recently I read that Southern writers hold three traits in common—a sense of history, a sense of family and place, and a sense of humidity. Growing up in Louisville in the late 40s and 50s, all three were inescapable, especially the humidity of the Ohio River Valley. Louisville was a city, much smaller then, made up of distinct neighborhoods. Mine was Crescent Hill where Emmett Field Elementary School, St. Mark's Episcopal Church, the Crescent Theatre, Weisert's Drugs, the Louisville Water Works, and Nap's Market were all within walking or biking distance of our home on Pleasantview Avenue, where I lived from the age of four or five until after high school. Louisville was leaner, more compact—without suburban sprawl, without fast food chains, without strip development, without shopping malls. It was a place where residents, even kids, could safely take a bus downtown to catch a double-feature at Loew's, the Rialto, or the Mary Anderson, or shop at Stewart's Dry Goods or Rodes, at Kaufman's or W. K. Stewart's. Crescent Hill, except for commercial stretches along Frankfort Avenue, was mostly a residential neighborhood with long, tree-dominated streets of middle-class frame and brick houses, no two alike. The crescent in its name, my father explained, derived from its being the highest point along the interurban rail line entering the city from the east. Despite the tornado of 1974, the neighborhood is still largely an extended arboretum of shaded streets, of middle-class households (more gentrified now), which have not changed greatly—of cicadas rasping during the dog days of August, the smell of burning leaves in the fall replaced now by fat, black plastic bags along the curbsides—a world where everything seemed to radiate from the Water Works, especially the landmark water tower whose swollen tank (dismantled during the last decade) with its promise of stability and abundance rose above Frankfort Avenue like a tethered blimp.

After nearly fifty years, I can still name most of the neighbors on both sides of the street for a block or so, especially those who had kids. I can remember experiencing TV for the first time at Carol Johnston's, the dentist's daughter across the street. I can remember Dr. Richard Wiley, the U of L chemistry professor whose brainy sons Haven and Frank went on to academic primacy in the Ivy League. And Ed Hogan, my father's law partner, who once overpaid me about thirty dollars for mowing his grass when he came home flush and a little tipsy from an afternoon at Churchill Downs. I can remember grownups after dinner sitting in lawn chairs on the terrace behind our house as the lightning bugs rose—my father, Uncle Louis, my mother's brother, or Mr. Mercke telling stories until dark, their cigarettes glowing under the tall, ivy-clad elms that arched over the flowerbed where my uncle pampered his hostas. And Uncle Orin, my father's brother, a World War I veteran and retired pet store owner who lived in the house he inherited from his mother across the street. In his backyard, Uncle Orin set up a half dozen feeding stations for all the birds except starlings. Regarding them as pests, he used to trap and quietly dispose of them, rigging a draw cord from his basement window to trip a propped-up box under which he placed bait. And Mr. Mercke, the father of my oldest friend Robert, firing his shotgun out the attic window at midnight to celebrate New Year's.

I can remember playing war with painted metal soldiers among the roots of the big sugar maple in the Merckes' front yard, the same tree in whose shade we were photographed for a feature in the newspaper, six or eight of us, young entrepreneurs with our Kool Aid stand, selling Dell comic books and sugared water that stained our tongues. The same tree in which, I was recently reminded, we ignited the nap of Robert Mercke's plaid shirt firing match guns made from clothespins, forcing him to drop down from his perch considerably faster and sooner than he'd planned to. There is also a cover photo for the Halloween issue of *The Courier-Journal Magazine* (October 23, 1949). The photographer captures five of us (plus one collie) trick-or-treating at the Merckes' opened front door. My sister Treva is tricked out as a masked gypsy; Robert Mercke wears a skeleton suit; two others, masked and unidentifiable now, wear similarly gaudy costumes—one looking a little like the straw man from *The Wizard of Oz*. Hatted, a bandanna across my nose, cap pistol drawn, I am peering over the skeleton's shoulder, masquerading as a cowboy. The collie, eyes yellow and eerily aglow, has come simply as herself.

Buzz Taylor at Kentucky Military Institute, age eighteen.

At the end of Springdale, the street that angled behind our house into Grinstead Drive, was Seminary Hill, the steepest and nearest high ground in the neighborhood. After every snow, we dragged our sleds there, sliding and fighting pitched snowball battles until our feet numbed or darkness came. The slope was punctuated with huge mock-orange trees whose fruit, in the appropriate season, we used to throw at each other, usually in fun. Each of us, at least once, collided against those trees as we caromed down the hill, sometimes on our American Eagles, once or twice on an unwieldly car hood or a deconstructed cardboard box. Addicted to activity, we often joined the night skaters on not-too-distant Cherokee Lake.

My mother, Dorothy Dey, had been raised in the house we lived in. Her father, William G. Dey, worked for the city, and his office was in the City Hall annex. Until my paternal grandfather died in 1916, my father and four

9

preceding generations of his family had lived on a farm at Worthington in eastern Jefferson County. He came to Louisville by way of Pewee Valley and finally to Crescent Hill when his mother gave up the farm, a part of the land acquired by my great-great-great-grandfather, Capt. Reuben Taylor, who had served six years in the American Revolution. For many years I assumed that the 4,000 acres of land he was granted for his services was the land on which he lived. I later learned that the grant was for land in Ohio and would have required his moving. Instead, he sold the land and used the proceeds to improve and extend the land he already owned. He and several of his brothers and cousins had immigrated to Kentucky from Orange County, Virginia, and several settled in the Worthington area. Until my grandfather's death, my father lived on the family farm on Chamberlain Lane at the end of Wolf Pen Branch Road. His most vivid childhood memory, amazing to me now, was accompanying his father to Louisville driving a herd of cattle along Brownsboro Road, then an unpaved dirt thoroughfare, to the Bourbon Stockyards in downtown Louisville. Our next-door neighbor on Pleasantview was George Mercke, whose son Robert, a year my junior, was one of my closest boyhood friends. His father, my father's friend, was also raised on a farm, this one in Crescent Hill off what is now Crescent Avenue. As he described it, the farm backed up on St. Joseph's Orphanage, celebrated during my teenage years for its annual orphan's picnic at which all of us could gamble either at bingo or the large, numbered wheels from which a winner could expect a return of fifty cents or so for each lucky nickel invested. Mr. Mercke, who had dozens of stories about Crescent Hill in the 10s and 20s, told a tale about raising prize game cocks, mostly Bantams and other exotic varieties, with which he yearly won prizes at the State Fair. This continued until a jealous competitor bought his entire stock for a handsome sum, exacting the additional pledge that Mr. Mercke, barely into his teens, bow out of future competitions.

A perennial draw in the neighborhood was the Crescent Hill swimming pool near the city reservoir, an acre or so of chlorinated water complete with high dives, bath house, and a concession stand where we snacked on Nehi oranges and popcorn for less than a quarter. At the shallow end of the pool, I learned to swim under the instruction of one of the tanned guards who gave lessons in the evenings. During July and August, we rode our bikes to the pool, paid a quarter or so, and spent the day diving and swimming, sunning ourselves and splashing each other until the shadows fell across the water and we pedaled home to dinner—relaxed, sunburned, deliciously exhausted. The preferred outfit for us during these idyllic summers was white (unlettered) T-shirts, elastic seersucker shorts striped blue or brown, and dark, high-topped tennis shoes.

Another key attraction was the Crescent Theatre, which over two decades took on a number of incarnations, first as the place each Saturday afternoon where we watched double-feature westerns—Alan Ladd, John Wayne, Randolph Scott. Preceding the feature was a serial (*Last of the Mohicans*, *Flash Gordon*, or *Dr. Fu Manchu*), which always ended with a cliff-hanger to lure us back next week. Later, as television pared the audiences down, it became an art theatre where I saw my first foreign film—the French thriller *Diabolique*, whose image of a drowned woman submerged in a bathtub is with me still. When the market for *bona fide* art films petered out, the Crescent became one of Louisville's seedier purveyors of adult "art" films, finally evolving into an upscale brasserie where one could eat and drink while watching Marx Brothers comedies. More even than books, the Crescent was a great nourisher of the imagination—the broad range of possibilities engendered when one entered that transforming darkness redolent of popcorn to plump down in one of the hinged, cushioned seats, a blue wedge of light illuminating the oblong screen as the red, plush velvet curtains were drawn. Watching a B-western or a swashbuckler at the Crescent—or occasionally the Vogue in St. Matthews—became a weekly ritual for my brother, my sister, and me. Weaning ourselves somewhat in junior high, we attended Mrs. Choate's dancing school upstairs above the theater, learning the foxtrot, tango, and hokey pokey—necessary steps in our emergence as the last generation of pre-rock ballroom dancers. What of course Mrs. Choate actually taught with varying degrees of success were courtesy and social confidence between the sexes, as well as physical coordination and a glimpse of ordered civility. Down Frankfort Avenue two blocks, I can remember the small but bustling Crescent Hill Library, where I attended children's programs during the summer and systematically checked out Joseph Altsheler's frontier adventure books, eventually graduating to *The Grapes of Wrath* and *East of Eden*—everything I could lay my hands on by John Steinbeck whose work, then, bordered on being racy.

My most prolonged ritual in the neighborhood centered on a quest for comic books. I knew the day of the week on which they were delivered to each drugstore—at Weisert's (which also served a mean cherry Coke at its ivory marble fountain and was located on the same block as the Crescent), at Hinkebein's and Wobbes' (businesses that still retained their apostrophes). Further east on Frankfort Avenue, at Bollinger's near the Water Works, where Mr. Bollinger, the ancient pharmacist, amid his jars and potions seemed, and was, a throwback to the last century and appearing to step out of a caricature of a Dickens character. Comics were a dime, and I collected and traded all kinds—Dells that featured Donald Duck and Little Lulu when I was younger, Entertaining Comics (E. C.'s) when I was older—whose *Tales of the Crypt*, *Frontline Combat*, and *Two-Fisted Tales* represented the best in illustration and boasted some historical authenticity in their accounts of battles and sagas. When they appeared, I snapped up the first dozen or so issues of *Mad*. Each of the numbered *Classics Illustrated*, more expensive at fifteen cents, I collected avidly until my mother made me store the bulk of them in a big trunk in the attic. By then I had well over a thousand, some of them collectors' items today. When I went off to college, they likewise were—to my agony and my mother's relief—quietly disposed of.

Just west of the Crescent Theatre on the corner of Birchwood and Frankfort Avenue is St. Mark's Episcopal Church, a modest stone building in whose sanctuary I spent most Sunday mornings until I graduated from high school, at first as part of the boys choir (with envelopes each month containing a dollar to sweeten our commitment) and then as an acolyte, wearing a starched white robe and sometimes red vestments, marching in the processional toting the heavy brass cross on its standard. On Sunday evenings we attended the "Young People" socials at St. Mark's, where we danced, I kid you not, to Glenn Miller on the hi-fi. I can remember the outrageous hats of the matron who decorated the church each Sunday and functioned as a kind of self-appointed arbiter of propriety, giving genteel salutations to each parishioner from the foremost proprietary pew. And Reverend William "Bill" Langley with his resonant, sermonizing voice. And Mr. Hobbs, the stern but gifted choirmaster who walked, or chorused us, through each week's hymns—and, typically, an ambitious Bach anthem—for two hours on Thursday afternoons, longer for special services at Christmas and Easter.

In the basement of the adjoining church building, Boy Scout Troop 319 met on Wednesday evenings. Each of us in our olive uniforms and spit-shined shoes would toe the straight, white line painted on the concrete floor where Sam Kelly, a former army sergeant, would inspect us and introduce activities—knot tying, first aid, the fireman's carry, even elementary cooking. Each summer we turned native for a week at Camp Covered Bridge in Prospect, and several times a year we would camp at nearby McGuire's farm where four of us, good friends (Robert Mercke, Stanley Schultze, Edgar Straeffer, and I), carried on the camping tradition for years after the quasi-military discipline and restraint of Scouts wore off. One of our legitimate scout trips was a survival exercise where each of us, equipped with an army-issue box containing bouillon cubes, Hershey Bars, waterproofed matches, and water purification tablets, had to make it on our own for a day or so.

On another outing we made the news when a member of our troop, in clearing a campsite, encountered what appeared to be a harmless snake. Disobeying all the cautionary training we'd received (non-poisonous snakes have round heads, poisonous have triangular heads), he extended his hand to pick it up, and the snake, a copperhead, bit one of his fingers. Scoutmaster Sam Kelly went into emergency mode, directing us in improvising a litter to carry him up the steep hillside to the cars. Tearing off down U.S. 42 to the hospital, he was accompanied most of the way by the obliging siren of a state trooper. The index finger of the snake handler swelled up to the size of a billy club. Later that week, a story and accompanying photo appeared in *The Courier-Journal*, the survivor grinning from his hospital bed.

After outgrowing the uniforms and the regimen of meetings and merit badges, we still took to the woods, returning to the same spot on the creek where we'd camped as members of 319. Now we came to drink beer and shoot our 22s. On the banks of the creek among stinging nettles we cleared another space with our machetes. Over a period of weeks we dug a hole about twelve by twelve feet and four or five feet deep, adding a corrugated tin roof and a woodstove so that we could camp on weekends. At night we told jokes and drank contraband beer; during the day we shot our 22s and ate Dinty Moore beef stew. We abandoned "the hole" when we found it flooded one spring with spillover from Harrod's Creek. Sometimes we canoed miles up the waterway from the mouth of Harrod's Creek. Once we spent most of a day building an unstable raft, lashing several logs together. I remember that day because a 22-caliber bullet fired by one of my messmates ricocheted off the water and drilled a neat hole in the seat of my pants. During those weekends we felt ourselves responsible and free—though not necessarily in that order.

Now we realize how fortunate we were in not having shot each other or seriously injured someone hiking through the woods.

Within walking distance of home was Emmett Field Elementary School, named for a circuit court judge whose stately old Italianate home still stands on Crescent Avenue. When I was ten or twelve, I enlisted to join the school safety patrol and "guard" the crosswalks on Stilz Avenue across from Nap's Market. Each morning three members of the faculty—Mesdames Waterman, Carson, and Booker—all career teachers of middle years and formidable presences—rode by in a lime-green '51 Chevrolet which I saluted each morning, a salute they sometimes acknowledged with an indulgent wave. One of the three, a "battle ax" who "advised" the student council and was a little neurotic about distractions and disruptive noises, instructed the student representatives to impose a penny fine for each pencil dropped in her classroom. Later, the action had to be rescinded because one of my classmates, nervous herself and prone to dropping things, owed a levy of five dollars after the first week. Infractions of discipline were severely dealt with, a lesson I learned vicariously when my kindergarten teacher, an otherwise loving and model instructor, confined one of my fractious, red-haired classmates in a chicken wire cage, which she, maybe with the janitor's help, had constructed in the middle of her classroom. I can remember Miss Crenshaw one day exiling me from the classroom to the hall for some forgotten offense and forgetting to fetch me. After lunch, toward the end of the school day, she was surprised to encounter me still sitting in my assigned hall chair, thumbing through an encyclopedia—what may have been my most productive day in elementary school. I can remember the dark, earthen-floored basement-shed under the school where we stored our bicycles during school and the playground where we played dodge ball at recess, an area that doubled during the summer as a park, nameless so far as I know, adjacent to the Louisville Water Works. And my short-lived career playing the French horn in Mr. Markart's school band—ending when my parents could no longer tolerate the dissonance of my practicing at home.

When school was out, we organized our own pre-Little League hardball games on the diamond near the school grounds. During summer afternoons near the park pavilion, we played games of cutthroat croquet or listened to stories read by the park supervisor, usually a high school co-ed or college student employed for the summer. In our early teens we bought bean shooters (now outlawed) and packages of navy beans from Nap's, staging massive beanshooter battles from which we all, miraculously, escaped unblinded. Whatever else it was, Crescent Hill was a child's paradise, a familiar environment where kids could act out nearly every whim and fantasy with near impunity.

Not so long ago, my mother, clearing out one of her closets, excavated some photos taken during the time my father was reaching adulthood in Crescent Hill. One was a standard team portrait with three rows of young men, helmetless, wearing aqua-blue jerseys, some of them grinning self-consciously, a few glaring defiantly into the camera lens. This was the Crescent Hill Athletic Club team, one of the post-high school, neighborhood teams that thrived in every area of Louisville. According to my father, they were fiercely competitive, fiercely partisan, sometimes recruiting bruisers to bolster the line or sweeten the backfield. The first row sat cross-legged, the second kneeling, the third standing with hands behind their backs. To the rear of them were backyards and two-story frame houses on Eastover Court, which backed up on the Emmett Field playing ground. The studio had softened the masculinity of the scene, color-tinting each roofline—baby blue, pale lavender. Rising above them is a single, stark, cruciform telephone pole. In the foreground is a football with "1929" chalked on the leather. My father—playing end my mother told me—stands obediently in the third row, third from the right, without shoulder pads and none too hefty. Instead, he wears a good-natured, though not thoroughly committed, smile—the Great Depression, law school, and fatherhood still ahead of him—his collective and individual identity, with Crescent Hill behind him, confidently intact.

A Wet Christmas

Buzz Taylor was a man of regular habits. He was up with the birds, off to the office by 7:15 AM, home by 5:30 PM unless on rare occasions he was held up in court by a deliberating jury or something had come up at the office. Seldom did he depart from his routines. A defense lawyer, he was accustomed to schedules and deadlines set by judges and the *Kentucky Rules of Civil Procedure*. As might be expected of someone whose working life centered on gauging cause and effect in terms of legal consequences, he favored the predictable over surprises.

Attuned to these patterns, my mother, who managed the household and much of the messy randomness of rearing three children, miraculously had dinner on the table at 6:00 PM each evening, feeding Buzz, her bachelor brother (my Uncle Louis), my older sister, younger brother, and me substantial meals that spared neither butter nor calories—a meatloaf, roast, pork chops (Welsh rarebit on Fridays for my uncle who was a reformed but residual Catholic who shunned fish). Born and bred a city girl, my mother served the hearty fare of the country—plough food that for some reason did not turn us all into blimps. Though the locus of dinner might be changed to the back porch during the summer months, especially before air-conditioning, the routine always remained the same, as though the schedule were cut in cuneiform on a clay tablet unearthed among the Sumerians. The pattern was ritualistically set, except for once a year—no more, no less—as offices and courts slowed down or closed in the days before Christmas.

Unlike more than one of his partners, my father was only a moderate drinker. I can say this with authority because for a time, I clerked in his office while I studied at the Brandeis School of Law at the University of Louisville. My gift to the Commonwealth, not known to me then, was not to enter the practice of law. One of my jobs at the office was to drive Henry V.B. Denzer home at the end of the workday. A lumpy, scholarly-looking man who wore bland suits and unenviable ties, he won most of his cases but never through personal charisma. Capable as he was as a trial lawyer whose bread and butter was automobile liability cases, he did not drive, never had. Blind in one eye from a childhood BB gun accident, he was a certified expert on insurance law as it affected negligence in accident cases. He knew, my father attested, as much on the law of negligence as any man in Kentucky. He also possessed a very dry humor. When the receptionist and secretaries at work would gossip and guffaws could be heard in the outer office, Mr. Denzer would stick his head around the door, roll his glass eye, and bellow, "What's all this frivolity?" No one was the least bit intimidated, nor did he mean them to be. Not marrying until late middle age, Mr. Denzer would have me accompany him to the Delta, a bar and restaurant at 434 Market Street, a block and a half from the law office, the third floor of a three-story building overlooking several magnolias and the east elevation of Gideon Shryock's classically designed Jefferson County Courthouse.

The proprietor of this watering hole for the courthouse crowd, Buddy, who then tended bar himself—though aided by two waitresses, Joanie and a redhead known as "Shively Red"—knew the tastes of his patrons, and almost as soon as Mr. Denzer stepped off the street and entered this dim-lighted refuge, there was not one but three or four double-double bourbons queued along the polished surface of the long bar where he was wont to stand or sometimes perch on one of the high-backed stools placed there for weary barristers. Eyeing those about him, some through what he could see reflected in the beveled mirror with its tiers of bottles behind the bar, Mr. Denzer would tilt back his head, his walleye fixed on the ceiling, and suck down his bourbon with perhaps just a whisper of water in one long draught as he commented on a case or shared a howler: "Why wasn't Jesus born in Letcher County? Because they couldn't find a virgin or three wise men in the whole county."

Most of the regulars were lawyers—Johnny Knopf, Henry Sadlo, Henry A. Triplett, Walter Redmon, Thruston "Redbird" Crady, and Chester Allen Vittitow, who always carried breath mints and once went home from the Delta and tried, unsuccessfully, to give his dog a haircut. Toping one night at the old Pine Room on River Road—a favorite suburban watering hole—Chester sang song after song at the piano bar with Mabel, the bar's longtime performer. His wife commented to Mabel on Chester's cavernous memory that permitted him to remember all those lyrics. When he excused himself to visit the loo, Mabel leaned over to Chester's wife and quipped, "Yes, he knows all of the words but none of the tunes." All of these men, except my father, savored a taste at the end of the day.

Often as he held forth reporting how some witness let slip a word that won or lost a case or quoting the judge's ruling on some motion for summary judgment or a directed verdict, the phone would ring and Buddy would pick up.

"Yes, Mrs. Denzer," he would intone dutifully, the soul of solicitude. "Yes, ma'am. I'll see if he's still here."

Of course, he was. Buddy, a man who honored his customers' right to privacy and a nip or two after working hours, would cup his palm over the receiver and catch Mr. Denzer's attention, asking if he were still there.

"Tell her I left ten minutes ago and am heading straight home," he would perjure himself saying, downing whatever remained of his unemptied glasses before finishing whatever he was holding forth about and settling up. "Better go," he would mutter to those within hearing, speaking with the resignation of a demasted sea captain facing the Spanish Armada. Then I would drive him to his home in the suburbs.

My father was not a big drinker, nor did he have much time to linger at downtown bars. But what about his father, the last full-time farmer of generations of farmers? Not that came down to us in family stories—with one exception. When my father was about ten (about 1915), he accompanied his father by horse and wagon (amazing to me) along the old Brownsboro Road and Frankfort Avenue to the hay market in downtown Louisville. What his father was transporting or selling he did not say—or I don't remember—but my brother informed me he was in fact driving cattle and that they were taken not to the old hay market but to the Bourbon Stock Yards. From the family farm at the end of Wolf Pen Branch Road on Chamberlain Lane to downtown Louisville must have been at least twelve or so miles, taking most of the day to travel. What I do remember is his saying that it was the dead of winter and very cold, and that on the way home his father stopped at Bauer's, the well-known restaurant-bar that had been a stopping place for travelers since the third quarter of the previous century. His father led him into the bar, and the barkeep asked what he would have.

"A shot of straight whiskey," my grandfather said, "and something less strong for the boy." This meant some predecessor of Coke or something like sarsaparilla or root beer.

And that was all I knew about family drinking history with the exception of my great grandfather, Philip Richard Taylor, a farmer and one-term state legislator who lost his seat in the General Assembly after failing to attend the session that voted on his local option legislation because he was hung over from libations sponsored the night before by representatives of the distilling industry. The bill lost by one vote, thus ending his political career and thwarting the desire of his teetotaling neighbors.

Whatever the case, my father was not a regular at the Delta. When Mr. Denzer would try to cajole him to come for a drink or two, he would make excuses except for what became his yearly exception. "What's training for," we would say today, "if not to break it occasionally?" His excuses were that he had something more he had to do at the office or something he had to accomplish on the way home—gentle perjuries. Neither priggish nor intolerant, he acknowledged the need, and the legal right, of others to take the edge off the day. Fact was, he was even-tempered and showed little of the tension that beset his partners. Alcohol was not for him the elixir of life. If anything, nature, wild or rural, was. My own brief experience was that most of the fraternity of lawyers I encountered, especially trial lawyers, were either neurotic or alcoholic, or both, by age forty. There was a great deal of pressure on them that could only be released with a drink or two.

But once a year, and just once, almost always in the days before Christmas, at 6:00 PM my father's seat at the set table went empty, the rest of us seated, potatoes steaming in their bowl, gravy cooling in its cradle, spinach marinating in its liquor, my mother at first looking concerned and then a little exasperated as the truth dawned on her.

"Where's Buzz?" my uncle would ask abstractly. And no one offered an answer though my mother and sister Treva had a good idea.

As the minutes clicked toward the six-thirty news with Walter Cronkite, my mother would roll her eyes and do what she could to hold the meatloaf or roast or whatever it was on the kitchen stove, eyeing the reliable clock on the wall as the minute hand descended toward its nadir at 6:30, then slowly rise toward its zenith at 7:00. She would wait as many tolerant minutes as she could, then tell us to eat before the food got cold. When we'd scraped the last green bean from our plates (which we were expected to clean), she would clear the table and begin washing dishes without my father, his dish towel in hand, a job he dutifully fulfilled after each suppertime.

Then, at 7:00 or a little after, we would hear a fumbling at the front door.

In would step my father, a little flushed, vaguely apologetic, grinning. My mother, never a nag, acted as though everything was normal and helped him hang up his overcoat.

"Oh, Buzz!" she would finally say, not really scolding, more resigned and relieved than angry. He offered no explanation, no excuses, as though this breach of implied promise was not really an infraction so much as a slight deviation from the norm, one to which he was entitled. His flushed face told the story. Keeping his natural dignity despite the tie misaligned in the open V of his collar, he would seat himself at the empty table, his children off doing homework or watching Milton Berle, Jack Benny, or *The Lone Ranger* on our first TV, a Motorola in a bulky wood cabinet at whose center was a smallish screen, its surface almost perpetually a blizzard of snow, the rabbit ears of its crude aerial requiring constant, subtle adjustments. Now it was his own screen that was snowy, a little blurry. My mother, in the kitchen, continued washing the dishes, recruiting one of his children for duty with the towel.

Never a boisterous drunk like some of his friends and members of the legal brotherhood (he could name the women who practiced law in Louisville on one hand), he had no time for prattle and courthouse gossip. Alcohol didn't loosen his tongue. Yes, during the winter evenings of early dark, he savored a glass of red wine before dinner, often a carefully prepared gin and tonic during the sweltering months of summer. Occasionally, if there was a social event—a game of poker or Buck Pitch on the back porch, he might indulge himself with a Miller High Life or a Manhattan, the latter maybe a carryover from the time during his college years when he waited tables at a New York City nightclub. Predictably, each Christmas he edged my mother from the kitchen so that he might concoct his famous eggnog, real eggnog, with fresh ingredients, egg whites, heavy cream, sugar, Myers dark rum and brandy, topped off by sprinklings of nutmeg in each poured mug that specked its milkshake-thick liquid a stippled brown—an eggnog that bore no resemblance to the pale surrogates sold now at Kroger.

For him, alcohol, seldom and sparingly consumed, served as a seal of contentment. The year was winding down, and things looked pretty good. There were challenges and obstacles ahead, certainly, but he could worry about them another time. Mint-flavored gumdrops clustered in a bowl on his desk at work, a large tin of peanut brittle at home. In the Frigidaire was the eggnog, the tree (a scraggly cedar with prickly needles usually cut on some farm he'd known from his Worthington days) decorated and lit, (presents decorously withheld and sequestered until Christmas morning), a fire in the grate—black locust he'd sawed on some desolate hillside with whomever he could conscript to lift and load, an involuntary but grudging servitude, starting with my brother and me. All was well. His daughter was a model student; his sons did not embarrass him often and showed occasional signs of gradual reformation from the world of lackadaisical studies and manic nightlife. His wife, my mother, was even-tempered and undemanding, tolerant to a fault. They knew each other's boundaries.

After his own warmed-over dinner, he would modestly ensconce himself in his accustomed armchair or stretch out on the sofa pretending to watch *Gunsmoke* or Groucho Marx, adrift in a state of mute euphoria. He wore a sheepish grin that assured us things were as they ought to be, even if he wasn't. If there was a UK basketball game, he would trudge up the stairs to bed, listening as long as he could to the tense announcements of free throws over the distant hullabaloo of Wildcat fans. If there wasn't, he would read himself to sleep over *American Horticulture, American Muzzleloader,* or *American Field Trials,* magazines that were his recess from the sterile prose of legal opinions, pleadings, and depositions. Never since childhood a churchgoer, though Christmas Eve would find his children in vestments choiring or acolyting in St. Mark's Episcopal Church where even the C and E Boys (Christmas and Easter) would make a showing, he would doze off and finally rise to climb the steps to bed.

According to my brother Doug, a day or two before our school break the weatherman forecasted snow. Never one to be impeded by the elements, my father retrieved the set of cumbersome tire chains from the basement and worked hours connecting them to the tires of his Chevy Bel Air, opting, for some reason, not to take his Willys jeep which had four-wheel drive. Next morning when he discovered that no snow had fallen, and there was not time enough to remove the chains, he dropped us off by school, the clanking chains creating a racket that embarrassed everyone but him.

He would be up early the next morning to peruse the morning edition of the *Courier Journal* as though nothing had happened. "Up and at 'em," he would hail us through our bedroom door an hour later, as if the day were an enemy that we must prepare to attack. That weekend, snowfall or freezing, he would make his annual pilgrimage to Worthington, the small farming community out U.S. 22 toward Brownsboro (where he, his parents, and siblings now lie) about ten miles from downtown Louisville, the farming neighborhood whose fields are now backyards of an East End subdivision that were then countryside with farms he'd known as a boy with neighbors he'd known all his life—whose precincts would always be home to him. He prided himself on his ready self-reliance, always too glad to escape the desk chair and circumspect town life to which he was resignedly tethered. Dressed in khakis and olive Navy-surplus shirt (though a K.M.I. graduate, too young for one war, too old for the second, he never served) on that weekend before Christmas, he would steer his old mud-colored jeep with the orange hubs through Crescent Hill and east of the city, finding refuge no amount of alcohol could rival in the unbroken fabric of farms whose landmarks were familiar from boyhood, barren fields and shorn trees contracted into winter stasis. Parking, he would carry his clippers and a hank of clothesline straight to the tree he'd scouted that summer, shinny up to a mistletoe-ladened crown ("He can scramble up that tree like a damn squirrel," a friend would say), and surgically clip bunches of the berried pagan magic and lower it to J.B. Myers or Mr. Mercke, his neighbor who came along because he couldn't bear to contemplate his friend falling. They would load enough in his old Willys jeep, his balance steady (and sober enough) into his late sixties to stock the neighborhood, a healthy clump hanging from the lintel that separated the living and dining rooms.

Eggnog, peanut brittle, car chains, jumbo clumps of mistletoe, stalled dinners—these were landmarks on my map of Christmas memories. The Delta is no more now. Better practices and more vigilant policing have curbed most of the excesses of Delta-goers. And those who go off the deep end—if they have no law clerk to drive them home—have a DD (designated driver) or recruit someone to summon a reliable taxi to ferry them through the Yuletide season, unscathing and unscathed.

Guineas and Griddle Cakes:
Two Portraits

An old photograph of Cousin Lucy shows her astride Nell, the pet mare she loved to ride around the farm. In those distant 1930s, the farm consisted of about 140 acres. It was located off Lime Kiln Lane in eastern Jefferson County about eight miles from the Louisville city limits. Wearing a sporty slouch hat whose trimmed-back brim makes it seem somehow an abbreviated version of a man's, she is in quarter profile, dressed in an old sweater and sort of riding jumper with buttons both at the neck and at the calves of the billowing leggings. One low-heeled shoe is visible, hooked into the stirrup. A child of the twentieth century (though she was born in the nineteenth) she sits on the mare like a man, not being content to ride sidesaddle, as was expected in her youth. She is in her mid-to-late fifties. The face, tilted down toward the reins in her left hand, is mostly shaded, her right hand resting on the pommel. The shadows over her full cheeks and pert, slightly upturned nose mask what seems to be a smile. Behind her is a snarl of branch ends encroaching into a milky sky. Other limbs from a tree in the background seem to rise out of Nell's bony head almost like antlers, the bit and bridle segmenting the mane and upper neck in neat geometrical plats. Long, frazzled wisps of timothy or fescue poke out of the field. Cousin Lucy and Nell dominate the landscape, as they do in memory.

Lucy Spurgin atop her pet horse Nell.

Not pictured is her sister Mony, whose name, rhyming with *Tony*, is a home-made diminutive of Edmonia. Edmonia Spurgin. When Cousin Frank snapped the photo of Lucy, Cousin Mony, as I was taught to call her, was probably in the kitchen. The kitchen was a pretty safe bet, for in kitchens she spent the better part of her life, if not by necessity then by inclination. The long, narrow room at the back of the house was her uncontested domain where she tirelessly prepared meal after meal, at first for Lucy and her brother Frank, then, after his death, for the two of them. Frank himself, dead before I was born, is a kind of cipher. He owned and operated a small printing company, but the only image I have of him derives from my mother, who remembered that both Lucy and Mony doted on him. After meals she could remember him retiring to a maroon leather daybed off the front parlor, where he would contentedly smoke his pipe. After Frank's death, his sisters usually sat at the small kitchen from whose window they could gaze out on the east side of the yard, which was punctuated by shade trees and a row of bridal wreath spirea against the whitewashed fence over which they could see pasture that sloped down the back of the farm.

Lucy Spurgin, 1930s.

Neither Cousin Lucy nor Cousin Mony ever married. Unmarried women in their generation were common, as was staying at home to keep house and look after aging parents. Their spinsterhood and the surname Spurgin were among the few characteristics they shared. Though both were ardent teetotalers, I remember Cousin Lucy in her later years sipping a glass or two of sherry at Christmas dinner. Both, it was said discreetly among my father's generation, soured on alcohol because none of their brothers, except Frank, ever "amounted to much." Several of them, I later heard, had drinking problems. Besides Frank, I can name only one other brother—Finas—named because his parents intended him to be the last. But that was before the birth in 1882 of Lucy, who supplanted him as the youngest child. She, Mony, and their four or five brothers had been reared near the small town of Eminence in rural Henry County, Kentucky.

Both were members of the Methodist Church, though by the time I knew them age and distance kept them both from attending very often. I have one vivid memory of a pie supper under sugar maples at the plain white church that fronted Old Brownsboro Road. I can remember long tables and folding chairs, and men in their shirtsleeves—old men, most of them, browned and creased from years laboring in the fields. They stood in twos and threes while the women sat in sociable groups, filling their plates only after the men and children had been served. My parents' car, a black 1948 Chevy sedan, was pulled off in the churchyard, its bulbous fenders shining under the trees. I must have been seven or eight. Cousin Lucy later told me of a wedding supper for one of the daughters of a local farmer, at which thirteen of the guests had died of food poisoning from consuming unrefrigerated chicken salad.

I have no other memory of them in church, partially because my father, who was closest to them, almost never went to church, preferring to cultivate the spirit with a hoe in his hand among the splendors of his garden. Partially, too, because age hindered Lucy's ability to drive her reliable Chrysler. Cousin Mony herself never sat behind a wheel, never had the desire to leave the farm. There were afternoons when we all went to Sunday dinner at the Old Stone Inn in Simpsonville, followed by my father driving them along the back roads that Mony and Lucy had known as productive farms during their childhood. Though tobacco and cattle were staples, the chief crop had been potatoes. As they passed each farm, they commented on the families that had lived there, many of whom had been buried for thirty years. Both, if such a question was not too personal, would profess conventional Protestant beliefs. Though they were very proper, neither was preachy or self-righteous. God was a benevolent absentee proprietor, always acknowledged but seldom mentioned, never a topic for discussion.

They bore little resemblance to each other. Lucy was small-boned and squat, but unusually animated. With her quick step and the habit of cocking her head to take in the world through clear, square-framed glasses, she exuded vitality and self-confidence. She survived the Depression among the employed as a school principal. Even without that income, one senses that Lucy and Mony could have simply retreated to the farm and sustained themselves as their forebears had, using milk money from the dairy for their few other necessities. Fueled by some hidden well of nervous energy, Lucy seemed always in motion. She had a businesslike mien and always looked everyone directly in the eye. She didn't walk, she traveled. My sister Treva described her expression as imperious, but I don't remember the slightest arrogance or harshness. With children, that look—a sternness she must have adopted as a school principal—could be unnerving. My cousin Mary Lawrence described her admiringly as "one stiff piece of rope." It's true that she had a strong sense of propriety, but she stopped far short of prudishness. I never heard her raise her voice or say a mean-spirited thing. Though she greatly admired both Roosevelts, she was naturally conservative in her view of things, having few good words for the social upheavals that followed the war. She was fit, always seeming much more robust than in fact she was, standing about five feet one or two. The contrast of her pale blue eyes and ruddy complexion gave her a scrubbed and healthy appearance even into her late seventies. Lucy, as the name denotes, was all light and energy. She was her own sun.

Mony, a decade older, was taller but very spare, thin to the point of frailness. She was pale, often appearing sallow, perhaps because she spent so much of her time indoors. Her arms, except when she rolled dough on the marble slab atop her kitchen counter, were always sleeved to the wrist, her dress always secured at the neck by a clasp or ivory-white cameo. She, like Lucy, wore thick, flesh-colored stockings and cobbie shoes with blocked heels. Her simple high-necked dresses were usually Amish gray or busy prints that resembled the speckled backs of her guinea fowls, birds in which she exhibited the most unapologetic pride. Neither she nor her sister wore skirts—only dresses. I never saw either of them in slacks. Naturally gentle though not overly genteel, she shunned pretense of any kind. It was true that when she dressed up in dark blue, she often wore a lace collar, a carryover from her mother's or grandmother's generation. I never in memory saw Cousin Mony wearing a bright color. Her natural backdrops were kettle gray and spatterware saucepans. Her shoulders were narrow and sharp, her collarbones protruding like folding wings. The skin hung loose on her face, and there was a dewlap under her chin. On the back of her left wrist was a kidney-shaped rust mark. Mild and unobtrusive, she wore her wispy dark hair on the back of her head in a modest bun, not so unlike the farm wife of Grant Wood's *American Gothic*, who was enough her contemporary to have been a schoolmate. She was a modest but incessant worker, and in her quiet way had something of Lucy's drive, expending that energy in household chores and stoking the kitchen range.

If Lucy was the queen bee, Mony was a contented drone. She was tranquil almost to the point of simpleness, but this was chiefly because she deferred to Lucy, through whose eyes she largely saw the larger world. Lucy's pragmatically conservative opinions were Mony's opinions though she seldom voiced them, content to let Lucy step forward as her proxy. In the outside world of politics, entertainment, and international affairs, she had little knowledge or interest. She was, as my father might say, "a gentle soul," an innocent in whose hands I never saw a book or magazine. In her deference to her younger sister, in her incessant activity and preoccupation with the practical details of daily existence, she was a throwback to the frontier, the rugged farming culture that she had been born to just seven years after the Civil War. She, unlike her sister, was very much at home in the nineteenth century and a little disoriented in the twentieth.

Outside the kitchen, her greatest interest lay in poultry, a vital link in the chain from production to consumption—what today we describe as a renewable resource. She and Lucy kept a sizable flock of White Rocks and Rhode Island Reds as well as a few paisley-backed Domineckers. Each morning she would gather eggs from the henhouse, a small building next to the tool shed whose flat surfaces were always floured with lime, giving the air a pungent chalky smell. To protect her eyes and pale skin when she was outside, she always wore a bonnet. From her bunched apron at feeding time she dispensed handfuls of shelled corn, summoning her chickens in an urgent, high-pitched mewing, "Here chick, chick, chick. Here chick, here." I have seen her shoo an aggressive rooster with a broom, indelicately swatting or even kicking it to underscore the message. From all quarters, fat pullets would rush to her, greedily pecking kernels from the grassless chicken yard. They would also eat from her hand, cocking their heads sideways to glare with one appraising eye before gingerly nipping the proffered gold. From these same plump layers each week she would select a candidate for the table. On the appointed day, C.W. Davis, their tenant and the only man living on the farm, would wring its neck, and she would pluck and dress it herself as a preliminary to the oven or skillet. Promptly at noon it would arrive for Sunday dinner in golden splendor on a platter.

But it was to the guineas—the speckled fowl that originated in West Africa—that she was most attached. My father described them as the wildest and most flavorful of so-called domesticated birds because of their gamy taste. He claimed that guinea cocks were the best eating birds, their dark meat the most succulent of all fowl, wild or domestic. And Cousin Mony not only shared this opinion but greatly abetted him in forming it. Despite the caterwauling of the guineas whenever someone drove up the gravel drive or when disturbed at night, she kept as many as two dozen, housing them in a large chicken-wire cage attached to the corncrib in the backyard. This wired enclosure was built several feet off the ground as a check against predators: the usual rogues' gallery of possums, raccoons, weasels, even the odd fox.

"Oh, they're better than watchdogs," Lucy liked to say. "They racket whenever anything comes into the yard."

As children, my brother, sister, and I were all attracted to what made the boldest appearance or, in this instance, the most raucous noise. We became students of guineas. As they ranged, we noted that they always followed a leader. The hens were so stupid they often led their keets through wet grass, where some would be lost while others succumbed to the chills that such forays were said to bring on. When tromping about the yard, they moved, my father used to say, "like a gaggle of nuns," hunched over and a little furtive in their motions. Cousin Mony's attraction went further. In her workaday-world, speckled print dresses sewn from flour sacks, she unconsciously flattered them by imitation. They were her totem. And, like them, she went her own way without much troubling anybody else.

Ten years younger and of a different generation, Cousin Lucy had a different temperament. Deciding to become a teacher, she had gone off to Columbia University before the First World War and earned both undergraduate and master's degrees in education. She had taught for a time before discovering her knack for administration. For several decades she was the principal of Cochran Elementary, the prestigious public school in downtown Louisville to which children of prominent downtown families sent their children, the sons in preparation for Louisville Male High. She was also a canny businesswoman, eventually owning a downtown parking garage and a quantity of blue-chip stocks. As for their speech, they both said "commence" for "start" and would do things "directly." They both pronounced "about" as "aboot," probably a carryover from the speech of their Virginia forebears. Living and working together virtually their entire lives, they formed a composite of home and career—one an industrious but demurring homebody, the other an entrepreneur; one with one foot in the nineteenth century mold of domesticity, the other striding confidently toward the liberated future that beckoned a generation of resourceful and competitive women.

My father, raised on a farm himself and a lifelong student of horticulture, kept his own large garden on the farm and maintained the adjoining orchard as well. In addition to the usual tomatoes, potatoes, pole beans, okra, rhubarb, and onions, he had an almost obsessive fondness for berries: raspberries, currants, strawberries, gooseberries, and several old-fashioned varieties of grapes. Not content with berries he could grow himself, he and Uncle Lawrence would go on blackberry-picking forays to undisclosed locations, bringing home gallons in a galvanized washtub. At midsummer when the vegetables came in, he would load up the jeep with baskets and distribute mounds of tomatoes, squash, and ears of Silver Queen to city neighbors—the produce coming in successive waves. They thought him a garden prince. He also brought my mother bucketfuls of snapdragons, bleeding hearts, coral bells, and antique columbines. When friends had parties, he would bestow this floral plenty on them. Spotting a bush of yellow roses in someone's yard one day, an old-fashioned variety he remembered from childhood, he stopped and asked the owners for a slip and successfully introduced it to his own garden. Whenever he could get away from the law office, he quick-changed into his army-surplus khakis, hopped into his mud-colored '46 Willys, and was off to "the country." This included almost every summer evening and weekend. As often as he could entice or dragoon us, my brother or I would go along, and some of the best hours of my childhood were spent wading in the branch, jumping from the barn loft into manure piles, or building "forts" out of cane and branches among the lichen-blotched boulders on the back half of the farm.

My father dwelled in two worlds, the button-down precincts of his professional life as a defense trial lawyer and his secondary, more open-collar existence as a husbandman, a grower of things, a nurturer, someone never more at home than outside the city limits on ground that resembled the farm of his childhood. At least once those worlds collided. As my brother Doug told the story, he once needed to petition the Kentucky Court of Appeals to grant him an extension on a deadline for a brief in one of his cases. His rationale for the extension was novel and compelling, and it must have raised some eyebrows, if not some humor, in a dry profession when he gave as his reason that he'd "lost his glasses in a brush fire." I can see the leather case with its clamp attached to his breast pocket slipping out as he swatted flames with a horse blanket or pitched buckets of water on black and smoldering grassland, a controlled burn that somehow escaped its jurisdiction and migrated to another. Original and straightforward as the request was, it must have moved the adjudicators, because his extension was granted.

He felt a special affinity for Cousin Mony and Cousin Lucy. They were living connections with the rural ways he'd given up for a career in the city. Though he would never confess it, he regarded himself as their protector. After each work session in the garden, he would look in on them. They loved to fuss over him, and we seldom got away without a snack of some kind, biscuits wrapped in a napkin or cold lemonade carried out to the garden where he would be hoeing, weeding, tying up beans, or scrunched up under the temperamental old Gravely mower that he used around the fencerows. They called him by his nickname, Buzz.

Cousin Lucy and Cousin Mony tended their own garden, a fenced, half-acre plot twenty-five yards or so from the kitchen door. Next to the garden gate was a work bell, its considerable bulk and weight ingeniously balanced on a single four-by-four post. "Never ring the bell," Cousin Lucy cautioned us, "because in the country, ringing the bell is the signal for fire or distress." That bell, its housing and four posts intact, stands now in the flower bed near my own house in the country. As the season progressed, Lucy and Mony both bent their backs in the long rows—planting, watering, weeding, and harvesting. Hauling water involved toting buckets from the pump that stood on a concrete platform next to the house, nearly thirty yards from the garden gate. When the canning began, the kitchen was converted into a mini-factory, filled with glass mason jars and lids that popped as they cooled on the crowded counter.

They could not have succeeded in the garden without the help of C.W., their tenant, a burly, thick-shouldered Black man, in his thirties then, who lived with his family in a modest one-story cottage just to the south of their farmhouse and close by the stock barn and one-room milk house.

He ran the dairy and did practically all the heavy work on the whole farm. His name was C.W. Davis, though he was always known simply as C.W. After Frank's death, and probably before, he worked under the watchful tutelage of Cousin Lucy. She called him C.W. He always referred to her as "Miss Lucy." Though I didn't think anything of it then, he was the first person of color I'd ever known. C.W. was a willing worker. He had a mild manner and natural dignity. He let me ride on the tractor with him. I never saw him angry, never heard him raise his voice except to stir one of the horses or chase a stray cow from the garden. He was a great favorite of my brother and me because he sometimes let us perch on the Farm-All with him or on the utility wagon when there was baled hay, fallen limbs, or manure to haul. Each spring, once the ground had dried sufficiently, C.W. would plow and disc the garden plot. Attaching a plow to the Farm-All, he would turn up the soil, leaving rows of darkly glazed furrows where the silver share had sliced.

It was no secret that Cousin Mony loved to cook. Preparing food was her art, her passion, the thing she could do best and from which she derived the most satisfaction and much justified praise. Her cornbread, cooked in a black iron skillet, was more than cornbread. It crumbled on the tongue. In it was just a suspicion of sugar—not sugar exactly but a kind of conspiracy of molasses and butter. Cooking for her was a form of speech, and she spoke its many languages. Never fancy or with rarefied entrees on her menu, her aim was to produce the best version of the ordinary. Her cooking crossed borders into unexplored regions of flavorings and toothsomeness. Though she was more than a fair hand at needlework and could sew with consummate skill, the allure of concocting a blackberry cobbler or frying a chicken with dumplings was more immediately rewarding. Unlike most cooks I've encountered, she was a light eater.

Following the example of those accomplished in other disciplines, she followed fixed procedures. For instance, after every meal, she re-set the table, placing plates and silverware as well as condiments on the small kitchen table or the "company" table in the dining room that adjoined the kitchen. This was not so unusual in itself, but she would cover the table with a second tablecloth, producing a white expanse of steeples and cones that resembled an imaginary snowscape in the Alps. Whether she did this to protect the dishware from houseflies or through some exaggerated sense of cleanliness, I don't know, but it was her undisputed way. It may have been a habit picked up from her own mother. A second was keeping the kitchen scrupulously clean, washing or wiping off in stages even while the meal was being prepared.

What was the connection between them and my father? We were blood relations through their mother Susan Spurgin, whose maiden name had been Susan Barrick, one of three daughters of a farming family that lived in then-rural Oldham County. Her sister, Edmonia Barrick, had been the second wife of my great-grandfather, Philip Richard Taylor, who had married Edmonia in the early 1860s. Both Cousin Lucy and Cousin Mony called me Dick, sometimes mentioning my grandfather's brother Dick— "Uncle Dick," my father called his great uncle, the ear, nose, and throat doctor—who had been a great favorite of Lucy and Mony's generation. Through Lucy and my father, I inherited a handsome Jackson press that her father, Charles Barrick, had made from cherry, probably harvested from his own woods.

Several family stories about Mony's kitchen have come down to us. I can vividly remember the antiquated wood-fired, cast-iron kitchen range that dominated one wall of her kitchen. It was Mony's altar, which she tended with great devotion. Next to it was a bucket always filled with kindling, and its ashes were carried out to what now is called a compost pile. Since the cook stove had no controls or gauges, she kept an even heat by lifting from time to time one of the metal plates on the stovetop to inspect the fire. The handle of her lifting piece had coils of springs around it to absorb the heat. Lifting the plates, she had an intuitive sense of how much heat the fire was producing and could add more wood or turn down the damper on the stovepipe according to her needs. She simply passed her hand over the opening and knew precisely what to do. In the commodious compartment next to the firebox she did her baking.

One Christmas, Cousin Lucy, thinking that she could lighten Mony's kitchen burdens and simultaneously introduce her to twentieth-century technology, bought a state-of-the-art General Electric stove, a white-enameled beauty with dials and knobs enough to satisfy the most fastidious chef. Cousin Mony thanked Lucy for her thoughtfulness and stipulated that she might still need her old stove for dishes that were especially ticklish. So the two stoves sat side by side in the kitchen, the one gleaming and unused, the other an anachronistic quarter ton of cast iron whose finish resembled unpolished gunmetal. Despite the labor-saving efficiency of the new range, it became obvious that Mony preferred the relic, which she kept reliably stoked with wood and performing in the old way. After a week or so when it was clear that Mony hadn't so much as boiled water on the new stove, Lucy asked why. Mony's response was that she knew it wouldn't heat properly, that it wasn't as predictable or efficient as her beloved wood-burner. Perhaps it was as much a matter of time. Mony knew how to pace herself on the woodstove, which demanded almost constant attention. This new appliance saved her too much time. Cousin Lucy finally removed it and gave it to C. W., and so restored the kitchen to its nineteenth-century purity.

The second story is by way of apologizing for not including the recipe of the dish it describes. On nearly every Saturday or sometimes Sunday morning, my father managed to find himself at the farm. When frost took the garden, he simply changed venues. During the winter months he would recruit several of us and go out to the rough, wooded slopes at the back of the farm to search for black locust, the hardwood he regarded as the best-burning. Despite the nuisance of thorns on its ropy bark, its density and heat value were unsurpassed; its straight-grained yellowish wood split easily. At other times we gathered walnuts, especially prolific on the big tree that stood on the edge of the woods in the lower pasture below the stock barn. Wearing rubber gloves to mitigate staining, using wooden mallets to split the lime-green hulls, a gang of us would fill a half-dozen bushel baskets and put them somewhere to season and dry for eating later. Many must have been grated into Cousin Mony's pies and salads.

Invariably, we were invited to have "a little something" for breakfast. One principle that Cousin Mony and Cousin Lucy both shared was an insistent hospitality that bordered on the militant. It was unthinkable for anyone to leave the premises without taking in a few calories. Just as in the Civil War when what began as a skirmish often heated up as a battle, in Cousin Mony's kitchen what began as a snack would quickly take on the dimensions of a meal. She liked to feed people, especially men, whose job it was on the farm to do work that was best done on a full stomach. Both Lucy and Mony praised appetites and were a little distrustful of light eaters. Simply stepping into a kitchen merited, at the very least, a steaming biscuit loaded with butter and grape jelly.

"Eat up," Cousin Lucy would say. "You look a little puny today." My father was particularly partial to Cousin Mony's hot water cornbread, a fried-in-bacon-grease griddle cake that is a German cousin to the conventional pancake. So taken was he with this dish that he deputized my older teenage sister Treva to visit Cousin Mony expressly to witness its preparation. Her charge was to bring the recipe home. All that was known beforehand was that water was used to mix the ingredients instead of milk. She did visit, but her mission failed.

"And how much butter do you add?" she asked.

"Just a little," said Mony.

Everything—bacon grease, eggs or flour—was a pinch of this, a handful of that. "Mix in some sugar," she would say, dolloping an indeterminate amount into the stoneware mixing bowl. Never three teaspoons or a quarter of a cup—nothing so precise. The amounts were not exact because Mony measured by habit from experience of eye and taste rather than by numbers or print on the page. She did own a battered old cookbook, but it consisted mostly of recipes exchanged with friends or cut out from newspapers and paper-clipped to the pages. Most of her recipes she carried in her head, and most of her art, unfortunately, went with her to the grave. Thus my father was frustrated in his effort to get a recipe for hot water griddle cakes at home, but that didn't deter him from enjoying them at the small, oilcloth-covered table in her kitchen.

In addition to chickens and the occasional guinea, she cooked veal and leg of mutton, sometimes a roast beef. In the spring she had us gather watercress from a wet, low area by the branch that meandered across the pasture. Washed and seasoned with a little salt and vinegar, it made a delicious salad. She baked more biscuits than bread, though cornbread was also a regular. My mother remembered that for supper Mony routinely served two kinds of potatoes, usually boiled Idaho potatoes and yams. She was famed for her desserts, especially her blackberry cobblers and the meringue that she served frozen with layers of raspberry sherbet. During the summer months she always kept a pitcher of ice-cold water in the refrigerator. I can still see the chill beads on the glasses when it was poured. In the garden there was always a plot devoted to melons, and I can vividly reconstruct the green vines snaking from the mounds, the flowering tendrils ballooning into muskmelons, watermelon, and cantaloupes. The following is a recipe for watermelon pickles, belonging to Cousin Mony and resurrected from my mother's store of time-tried favorites:

Watermelon Pickles

Select four pounds from rind or melon and cut in one-inch cubes. Weigh before putting in lime water. Soak two and one-half hours in lime water. Dry well, cover with fresh water, and let stand overnight. Drain next morning. Cover with fresh water and boil two and one-half hours until tender, adding water if necessary if it boils dry.

Lime Water Brine

two quarts cold water
two tablespoons lime (purchase in drugstore)

Vinegar Syrup

two quarts vinegar
one pint water
four and one-half cups sugar
two tablespoons allspice
two tablespoons cloves
ten small cinnamon sticks

Bring syrup to boil, add rind and boil two hours until syrup thickens. Pack in sterile jars, seal, and keep in a cool place. These are crisp and delicious. The main problem is finding a watermelon with a thick, white rind.

The succession of meals would have gone on indefinitely had not the century finally caught up with them. When Cousin Mony entered her eighties, they both knew it was time to move to town. Mony had broken her hip in a fall and afterwards had trouble getting around. Though she would never utter a complaint, she was in agony. She effectively hid her stiffness and altered gait, but there were other signs. Her meals became less elaborate, her cooking for company less frequent. Finally, Lucy bought a lot in suburban St. Matthews and built a one-story brick house designed for their comfort. They got on pretty well, though Mony's woodstove had been a casualty of the move and was left behind. By way of explanation, Lucy concocted several alternate excuses, namely city ordinances and fire insurance regulations. Storing and toting the firewood would also have been a problem. The truth was that Mony was tired, and C.W. was no longer around to help, since he and his family had moved to downtown Louisville, where for a time he managed Cousin Lucy's parking garage.

The farm was sold to developers, who soon dismantled most of the farming operation and converted the rolling fields into a suburban enclave. I can remember as a kid chasing rabbits in the front field behind a hay cutter while grownups pitched square bales onto the bed of a flatbed wagon. Now that field is a gridwork of barn-sized brick houses with black, oversized mailboxes, and manicured yards supporting exotic flora watered by elaborate sprays piped from the city reservoir. Neither Mony nor Lucy, so far as I know, returned to see the transformation. Neither, I suspect, had the heart to.

Things My Father Tried to Teach Me

"Hang it up!" "Keep it greased!" "Hook the gate!"—these were my father's mantras, his attempt to introduce me to the practicalities of surviving in the rural America of his youth. The first two items of this catechism related to his reverence for tools. In the country, his two-room shop—a frame, garage-like structure on a concrete pad—was full of tools, each in its place on pegboards within easy reach, festooning the walls, some stashed in the rafters, a place that smelled of motor oil, dried seeds, and fertilizer. After his death when the tool shed was emptied, I can remember someone quipping that he owned enough tools to equip a CCC camp—shovels, axes, pitchforks, mauls, hoes, sickles, spud bars, rakes, wrench sets, two-man saws—implements of all descriptions. With them he maintained a half-acre vegetable garden and the half-acre or so of what remained of the orchard that had been on the farm beyond my, and probably his, memory. The apple and pear and peach trees were pruned according to the library of horticultural books he collected at home and read for pleasure as much as instruction. He had a complete set of New York State Agricultural Experiment Station's *Fruits of New York*, a series of seven monographs on hardy fruits, famous for their striking color plates, as well as a couple of hundred books on growing things, a collection I could not bring myself to part with after he could no longer read them. Horticulture for a lifetime was his passion. When he came to make a career choice, he had initially aspired to become a landscape architect until he learned that the profession required drawing skills. He had no drawing skills, so by default he settled for becoming a lawyer. The irony was that on my mother's side of the family were several artists, his brother-in-law serving as art director of the Louisville paper, another brother-in-law a talented commercial artist whose son, a hunter, painted ducks for Ducks Unlimited and a fine portrait of Thomas Merton.

Yearly in the spring my father held his ritual of planting—garden vegetables, trees, shrubs, flowers—practical plants that were edible in his middle years, mostly adornment in the later ones. As he shoveled a hole for the fruit tree or thornless cane of a domesticated blackberry that came swathed in damp newsprint, I stood by teenaged and skill-less, with a bucket of water to which he added generous tablespoons of a green powder called Ra-pid-Gro. He made sure I followed every step of the procedure as if divining that I would never top Everest as a gardener, though I might become a planter of trees. He was prescient. I write this by a window gazing out at maples and dogwoods and magnolias, some of which I planted or transplanted forty-five years ago. My gardens have all been strangled by weeds, another way of saying by my own neglect. As he filled the hole and carefully tamped the dirt around the stringy roots, he would have me stir and slowly pour the green water from the bucket, giving the moistened skein of roots a good start in what would be their adopted home. "Hook the gate" must have been an admonition from his own childhood when an open gate meant chasing down wandering Holsteins or a strayed workhorse, a risk to be avoided.

His was a life of little departure from established routines. During the week, he practiced law in Louisville at 233 S. Fifth Street. From his third-story office window he could gaze down on the east end of the Jefferson County Courthouse, that elegant block-long structure designed by Gideon Shryock, the young man who introduced the Greek Revival Style in public buildings to Kentucky. *A man who could draw.* Weekdays my father stuck to professional dress, wearing the prescribed coat and tie, a suit on days when he had motion hour, a hearing, or, less frequently, a trial. On weekends he went native, pulling on old khakis and a work shirt, which made him resemble the retired G.I. he wasn't. Though he had graduated from a military high school, he was regarded as too old for active service during World War II. Having two children and another before VE Day and working for the government to boot, he clinched his draft deferral during the war. In both settings he was known as "Buzz" to those who knew him, only among those less familiar or more formally as Joe. Instead of dress shoes or loafers, he preferred wearing moccasins or something akin to what today we would call topsiders. To complete his transformation, he hopped behind the wheel of his 1946 Willys civilian jeep, a vehicle whose canvas top was removed each spring and whose windshield could be secured to the hood to confront the air head on, as he did most other things. During the summer his forearms and the V of his neck were a bright crimson, never tanning. In 1965 he replaced the jeep with an improved model, this one cherry red, in contrast to the drab mustard brown of the earlier model that resembled the vehicle in which John Wayne zipped among the palms in the Pacific theatre of the war.

Imagine smoldering on a hot day in June in the humidity of the Ohio River Valley. My father has recruited me on Saturday to put in a day working in "the country," Cousin Lucy and Cousin Mony's farm off Lime Kiln Lane. Knowing that I was not much of a hand at tedious jobs like weeding or hoeing—drudge work, unexciting—he has held out the prospect that I can mow the margins around his garden, especially where the fence is bordered on three sides by ragged pasture with its weeds and rough grasses that slope to the wooded creek bottom and rise again to meet U.S. 42.

The mower is an ancient Gravely, a heavy-duty machine with manly steel handles and an armature extending from the hooded housing of the engine with a sickle bar at the end, scissoring blades that slide back and forth on grease through pronglike guards that are supposed to deflect the thickest brush and keep the blades from jamming. When working properly, the blades make a snicking sound as I imagine a mad barber snipping incessantly at my ear. The snicks offered a countermeasure to the engine's incessant roar. Beneath the cylindrical gas tank, which my father always cautioned me to check before beginning, there is a wheel the size of a coffee saucer whose gray metal is worn to a silver sheen from the friction of years. In its slot is a leather strap with an eyelet in it that latches on to a catch on the wheel, creating the resistance necessary to propel the engine to life. It is wound around grooves so that when pulled, the engine will turn over, and gas will combust in the carburetor with an assertive growl. When pulled with authority and briskness, the engine, choke pulled out, will turn over and start. I have watched my father start it dozens of times and go through several false starts, jerking the belt so that just the proper thrust will fire the engine. From the other side of the fence, he pauses a moment to observe, leaning momentarily on the knob of his hoe. I wind the strap around the sprocket and pull, but the engine puffs and stalls, the spark plug not firing. It's an effort. Knowing that he's watching, I wrap it as I've seen him do as he yells for me to set the throttle a little higher to give it more gas and to wait a minute so as not to flood the engine. I do and try again. It kicks over but fails to catch. By now I am frustrated and wet with perspiration, my fresh shirt sopping in places, a runnel of sweat trickling down the valley between my bony shoulder blades. The moistness is an itchy moistness.

Sensing my distress, my father puts his hoe aside and walks down the fence line to climb the disused slatted gate too far from the nearer garden gate where he parked the jeep: "Never climb a gate except on the post end," I can still hear him saying. He wades into the swale of grass that rises about his knees, leaving a vague silver path through the fescue, grasshoppers rising as he plods. Without saying anything, he winds the strap and yanks it, applying the savvy of one who has experienced dealing with unreliable people and machines. Under his authoritative hand, this time it sputters and coughs but doesn't catch. He has forgotten my presence. He bends and huffs a little. I can see the white of the skin beneath his dark hair, mostly still intact over sixty. The competent arms extending from his rolled-up sleeves are summer crimson, dark blotches of sweat mapping his chest and underarms on his olive work shirt. Still not speaking but determined not to show his exasperation, he adjusts the choke as if to communicate with the balky engine. He methodically rewinds the strap around the grooved sprocket and pulls again. This time the engine responds with growling renewal, its roar between us deafening. He shouts for me take it from there, and I grip the clutch on the handle, releasing it gradually to avoid the risk of choking it out. With one hand he motions in a direction parallel to the fence and I make my first run, the snicking blades felling the tall stems and laying them in silver windrows. Conscious that he is watching, I put on my best show, keeping a straight line and not overaccelerating.

By the time I am cutting my second swath, he has turned his back and gone back to his garden, satisfied that he can turn his attention elsewhere. The heavy machine bucks over the uneven ground, the knobby braids of its tires bumping over ruts in the hillside. Through the vibrations thrumming through the handles, I can sense its precarious weight and know its power far exceeds mine. I can only give in to it, letting it go its way, occasionally turning it by lifting the handles, bearing down, and pivoting at the end of a row. Steering it and keeping its balance on the tilted grade is as much as I can attempt to do. Carefully, as much as I'm able, I steer it into the wall of thick grass and keep its balance, ranks of thick sedge and clumps of tough grass reduced like rows of advancing infantry on a battleground. Occasionally a stalk of towering scotch thistle bends under and spits cotton from its pink-flowered, spiky crown. The machine is a beast doing the work of brutes.

After a time, I feel the heat crowding me. To breathe is to raise a sweat. I feel an itchiness around the collar that makes me want to strip off my shirt. School is recently out, and I'm working on a summer tan. I've brought my sunglasses with me and put them on, switching them with my regular reading glasses, which I place in the breast pocket of my short-sleeved shirt. The glare is reduced to a comforting blur as the world transforms into a calmer, cooler green. *Where do I put the shirt?* And then I remember my father's mantra, "Hang it up." The pasture is shadeless, ablaze with penetrating light. There is nothing on which to hang the shirt except the garden fence, a woven wire job with a strand of barbed wire running along its crest to discourage the dairy cows that used to graze there. But the fence is uphill and maybe twenty yards away, much of the distance through high grass and buggy. Applying the primal reasoning of the American teenager, I think, *why not simply set it in the grass—grass already cut?* A moth drawn to flame.

Striking on this ready solution, I fold and carefully lay the shirt in the windrow with the glasses intact in their temporary home. My thinking is that the shirt will be safe, that I will not pass this way again and can retrieve it when the job is done and we are ready to leave.

So I unbutton the shirt, a creamy new chintz job that breathes, place it in plain sight on a pillow of grass, and continue cutting, dazed from the sun and the lulling drone of the engine as tall grass slips into its maw, and tremors of heat rise from the metal hood, wafting in a steamy haze. I can still feel the sun searing into my neck and upper back, my shoulders. I remember being told, probably by my father, that the word *redneck* literally meant those who worked and spent most of their time outdoors. I knew my white city skin would be burning that night. I knew that guiding the machine was more like corralling a fractious horse, control a comfortable illusion. As I rode it down the end of one wall of field grass and up another, I pivoted awkwardly to reverse directions, using the mowed grass as a guide to set my next course. After five or six long rows, I slipped into fantasies of the summer ahead—freedom from school, pursuing someone to date, camping with my friends from scouts, hanging out—maybe reading a paperback or two.

And then things changed abruptly. Under my feet appeared shreds of fabric that I recognized as the remains of my shirt. I cut the engine and stared at the strands of ripped fabric before I remembered the glasses. The frames don't matter, I told myself, but what about the lenses? For a moment I held out hope that the gods who governed grasses and glasses had spared them. In vain. Kneeling, I found one twisted plastic stem that was detached from what remained of the frame. Here I was also disappointed. Parting the mesh of mown grass, I caught a glint of light. Still attached to the frame was a lens with a crazed convexity through which no images would pass again.

"Hang it up" struck me like a shock the time I plugged in my radio while standing on the wet bathroom tile. A stab of guilt caused me to turn my attention to the garden. There, leaning against the fence, was the appraising gaze of my father. Our eyes met for a moment, and then he slowly strode toward the gate again, heading my way.

Approaching, he said nothing, looking first at me and then at the stilled mower and then at the pathetic ruins of my shirt. I was expecting curses or a general dressing down from an angry drill sergeant before a cowering recruit. I sensed that I'd dramatically ruffled his usual composure. Instead, I found a stoic in a sweat-stained shirt. He uttered not a word, slowly wagging his head from side to side, studying the strands of ripped fabric in the grass before looking up at me again. Words wouldn't come to me. I picked up the tattered shirt and placed it over what remained of my glasses. He looked at the shirt and then at me, slowly turning his head from side to side.

"You better find some shade," he finally said. "You look overheated." Then with a practiced hand he re-strapped the metal spool and started the engine on his first try. He finished out the row and ran a couple more for good measure and cut off the power drive. The snicking stopped, and he maneuvered the beast back toward the garage, spouting a plume of black smoke as he changed gears.

Then we both knew it was time to go. He closed the tool shed and climbed into the open jeep, its metal cool in the speckled shade of a massive elm by the orchard fence. The fence was lined with gaudy flowers, its border converted to a flowerbed. I climbed in, stowing the remnants I hoped my mother wouldn't see under the seat, where I would not have to look at them. I belted myself into the cushioned seat, and we were off, driving the eight or ten miles back to the city, hot air flowing against us in currents over the lowered windshield. I sat shirtless, still wearing my sunglasses though it was late and the shadows were lengthening.

"The glasses too?" he asked finally, turning his gaze from the road.

I nodded, holding my eye on the white line of the lane stripes as they zipped under the hood of that humming engine. As we approached Indian

Hills subdivision, the highway—a last stand of woods in the suburbs bordering either side—made a steep dip into a valley, descending maybe two hundred feet. We were struck by a wave of chilled air as though suddenly entering a cave, and I felt it course through my vulnerable, shirtless, sunburnt body, causing a dual sensation of burning and freezing.

To make matters worse, when he was explaining what happened to my mother, my father said that he had looked up from hoeing to see me heading for a patch of white in the windrow. He anticipated quickly what was about to happen. He put aside his hoe and rushed to the fence, desperately waving to get my attention when his shouts didn't reach me over the growling engine as I proceeded unfazed. Watching disaster unfold, he had shouted futilely, knowing I could not hear him over the thundering engine. Helpless, like all parents, my father had become the lead witness of his children's follies. This happened over sixty years ago when I was about fifteen, months shy of becoming a worry on the roads. What I remember from that ineradicable moment is the fact that he withheld tongue-lashing me, granting me a moment of grace before the crossing of stars that he knew would instruct me in the days ahead.

The Egg Gone West: A Late Elegy

David and I thrashed our way down the slope to the Kentucky River past skimpy water maples poking out of fissured limestone shelves. We waded through a mesh of driftwood and plastic milk jugs—and whatever other flotsam high water had deposited along the banks below Lock 10. We stepped over grayed barn boards that had drifted from the uplands of Eastern Kentucky, water and pop bottles, logs with puddles of rainwater in their cavities, a sediment of mud, caked and cracked, to the edge of the river. The surface had the sullen oily glow of day-old coffee. Across the river we could just make out the palisades of a reimagined fort, a pale imitation of the upraised logs that withstood a siege by British and Indians in 1778. Our boots broke through castles of twigs that had accumulated along the banks, and I feared stepping on a snake. Both of us stopped short when we spotted a hunk of water-sculpted wood half-buried in a latticework of sticks. We quickly saw that it was what remained of a monstrous tree. It was mapped with wavy black rings and mottlings that announced it was a sycamore. Rolling over this odd piece of symmetry among the off-scourings of the Kentucky River, we knew we'd found something. That was thirty-three years ago, the life span of Jesus.

The author, Gray Zeitz of Larkspur Press, and David Orr.

David Orr (1942–1989), my best friend and spiritual father, died of a heart attack in August of 1989. Teaching the previous school year in Denmark, I had been out of touch with him. The last I heard of him was a one-sentence postcard: "The egg and I have gone west." He had divorced his wife Monica, a bright woman from Louisville who shared his interest in books and the life of the mind. They had met in 1959 at a jazz festival in French Lick, Indiana, and married in 1964. I was best man at his wedding. In 1968 Monica gave birth to a daughter, Laura, and I was honored to be her godfather. The marriage lasted for two decades before the divorce. After their parting—before he left to start his life anew in California—David had asked to borrow what we called "the sycamore egg." We had found it a year or so before in a pile of driftwood on a rocky beach by the Kentucky River at the site of Fort Boonesboro, the crude stockade erected 200 years earlier by Daniel Boone and a company of bushwhackers. The fort was constructed under the direction of Richard Henderson, a land speculator whose proprietary company was aptly named Transylvania, "across the woods." Now the locale is a state park, the site of the original fort replaced by another stockade with a gift shop selling caps of artificial coonskin fur. Fort Boonesboro—the long-gone original—had been the first white settlement in Kentucky, the first fortification eventually being replaced by a Depression-era log imitation that had all the authenticity of the Lincoln Logs I'd played with as a kid. David and I had spent the morning exploring one of the creek beds that fed into the Kentucky, imagining ourselves members of a fictional company that David had christened The Kentucky Creek Walkers Guild. Our half-joking, impossible goal was to explore every creek in Kentucky, a state that has more waterways than perhaps any other in the country except Alaska.

A little larger than a beach ball, the "egg" had been buffeted who knows how far and for how long in the water, floating northwest from its starting point—probably from some caving bank at its headwaters in the northeastern uplands of the state. The currents had sculpted it into a wonky oval, a sodden ball of pulp. Though it could float, it was waterlogged and heavier than the two of us could carry. Imitating Sisyphus of Greek mythology, who was damned by the gods to roll a boulder uphill for eternity, we shoulder-pushed it up a steep slope to the road, somehow hoisting it into the back of my VW hatchback. From the river we drove it to the tenant house I and my wife Lizz rented near Athens,

Kentucky. The aspirational name Athens is pronounced with a long A, not to be confused with the Attican city-state that was the birthplace of democracy. This crossroads hamlet is eight or so miles east of Lexington. Once home, we set the wooden sphere out to dry. When it had bled out all the moisture it was going to, I saturated it with a concoction of linseed oil and paint thinner, followed by several coats of polyurethane to form a seal. A curiosity among our friends, the egg took on a kind of talismanic power for us, marking much more than our outing by the river. So I was not surprised when David requested a loan of this souvenir of our Kentucky explorations when he ventured west. What I realized only after his death was that "going west" was a euphemism for death during the First World War, a reference to passing from the planet in the direction of the setting sun, an expression probably used from the time of Homer.

My best friend had died at forty-seven of a heart attack in Berkeley, California. His primary life had always been mental, not physical. David had an absolute contempt for his body. He smoked heavily, he often drank too much and didn't unduly exert himself. Given to a kind of Mandarin rotundity, he was never obese. Never physically active, he more often could be found lying on a couch with book in hand. He looked healthier than he was. With thick dark hair and an olive complexion, he claimed some Native American blood in his lineage, maybe Cherokee—just enough swarthiness to make him seem a little more exotic.

I first met David when his family moved to my elementary school district in Crescent Hill. When his precociousness was recognized by our teachers, he skipped third grade, and we met as fourth graders at Emmet Field Elementary School. At the suggestion of our mothers, we joined a Cub Scout pack that met in a nearby church. For a time we followed, as Cubs still affirm, the law of the pack. But David was clearly not as accepting of conventional credos as the rest of us. Nor was he a compulsive joiner. His community was mostly inner. One other venture into the public arena was dancing school above the old Crescent Theatre on Frankfort Avenue between our homes, a ritual of the 7th grade when apparently our mothers decided that learning some steps in ballroom dancing might soften the savage in both of us. David's greater commitment was less public. From an early age he was an insatiable reader, a habit he may have picked up from his stepfather Jess or his mother Lois, their house full of books and high-calorie dinner table conversation about local causes and community well-being as well as art and politics. And no television, which later his favorite student of letters, Guy Davenport, described as the world's greatest invention for which no use has been found.

Born in Louisville, Lois Culter attended the University of Louisville, where she met Charles Orr, marrying him in her sophomore year. Only nineteen, she sailed off to Europe for their honeymoon. Among the other countries they visited was Nazi Germany. They were about to embark for India when they read of the revolution in Spain in the early days of the Spanish Civil War as fascist forces coalesced in a pact of conquest in a full-dress rehearsal for World War II. This was the period of Hemingway's *For Whom the Bell Tolls*. Politically, Lois was a radical socialist, living and working in Barcelona during the Catalan Revolution and the Spanish Civil War. Though not directly involved in the fighting, she was active in the Republican cause that resisted the Fascism of General Franco. A member of the Workers' Party of Marxist Unification female militia, she and Charles were eventually arrested but released after a month or so, even finding time to write a little book about her experience entitled *Letters from Barcelona: An American Woman in Revolution and Civil War*, published in England.

David's birth father dropped out of the picture early and thus was not a big influence on his upbringing. What his father did or where he lived—it may have been Chicago—I don't know because he was seldom, if ever, mentioned. Jess Cusick, David's stepfather, had vague jobs with state and local governments, gathering statistics, conducting polls, writing reports—a bureaucrat's bureaucrat. He appeared to me as a satellite of his strong wife—David's mother. By her first husband, Lois also gave David a younger sister, Elizabeth. After Jess came a brother, Benjamin, who died tragically, drowning as a toddler at Lakeside Swim Club in the Highlands. This death affected David and his family profoundly. It's difficult philosophically to account for such a death. David found some inspiration from his grandmother, Ann Culter, a painter who had helped form an organization with a name like the Louisville Art League, an organization that promoted art and artists in Louisville between the world wars. I own two of her paintings that David gave me when his grandmother died, one a bold portrait of a young man done in the bold simplicity and monumentalism of the Works Project Administration era.

David and I parted for a few years when his family moved to the Highlands, where he attended another middle school, but we reunited at Atherton High School (AHS) that drew students from both districts.

Together we joined a high school "literary" social Club, Sigma, a carryover from an earlier generation of so-called literary societies. Sigma did produce a literary magazine each year with articles and pictures of its members, but I don't remember either of us contributing anything. Instead, we concentrated on having a good time, going to parties and drinking illegal Pabst Blue Ribbon beers—having as wild a time as we could manage in cars we borrowed from our parents. And chasing girls. There were seasonal dances, and I can remember David shagging around a dancefloor with one girl or another, energetically bopping with his elbows out and mostly sitting out the slow dances.

Academically, David was off the charts, and he didn't have to work very hard to zap standardized tests and ace his classes, not only in the humanities, as you might guess, but in higher math and the sciences as well. Lapping up ideas and facts was a natural component of who he was, as inescapable as breathing. He was fueled by a passion to discover *the* answer to things, or at least a creditable explanation of our human predicaments or a guide to free ourselves from the societal tentacles he perceived around him. He experienced an envelopment of values and insights, a world of flashy shopping centers and the first drive-through burger joints on former croplands converted into vast parking lots, reflecting a constricting mindset that, to him and increasingly to me, spelled doom. Though his grades did not always show it, he out-tested virtually everyone in our class at AHS. In truth he was often bored, always carrying a book outside the curriculum that he could read instead of what was being taught, usually something he already knew. The book might be J.D. Salinger or one of the Beats or someone I'd never heard of, like Jean-Paul Sartre. Ferlinghetti was a favorite, or the classical cynic Diogenes or something on macroeconomics. He had a fondness for radical politics and anarchy, a devoted student of the Wobblies and "Big Bill" Haywood whose battle cry was, "Let's undo the done-for world and start afresh from chaos." Populism ("Raise less corn and more hell") and the American labor movement especially drew him as well as the folk music these movements engendered through Mother Jones, Pete Seeger, and Woody Guthrie. Among the poets that attracted him were modernists like Ezra Pound, William Carlos Williams, and James Joyce but also unconventional poets like E. E. Cummings or the quirky Lorine Niedecker, the latter a kind of contemporary Emily Dickinson in her homey originality. I learned later that his feats of reading were owing in part to his insomnia. Because he could not sleep, he read. I owe my love of William Faulkner's novels to him, though I confess my first reading of *The Sound and the Fury* was a washout, the only book I later recommended supplementing with *Cliff's Notes* or a reading guide.

David was also a natural teacher, and early on he set me to reading strong poetry and writing feeble lines masquerading as poems that must have kept him biting his tongue. He introduced me to poets not included in our standard high school literature text. Those anemic anthologies, wearing frilly Victorian aprons, did not extend beyond *The Genteel Tradition* and Carl Sandberg, ignoring such innovative modernists as T.S. Eliot and Ezra Pound. Even William Carlos Williams was too radically democratic for our teachers. One, an autocrat of the classroom who had taught my mother, insisted on keeping her feet in the tepid gentility of the Victorians. Next to the irreverent and radically experimental E. E. Cummings, a favorite was Dylan Thomas, whose lyricism in "Fern Hill" stirred within me a desire to write poetry: "Oh as I was young and easy in the mercy of his means, time held me green and dying though I sang in my chains like the sea." I had never encountered anything like this in my antiseptic high school literary anthology, and David was my enabler, bestowing on me a fat and tattered copy of Oscar Williams's *A Little Treasury of Modern Poetry* that became my bible. Largely at his urging, I kept lists of the books I read.

David also gave me the rudiments of social conscience, at one point during my senior year persuading me to read James Agee's *Let Us Now Praise Famous Men*, maybe the longest book I had read at the time. In 1937 Agee, a Southerner, had been commissioned by *Fortune* magazine to travel to northern Alabama to spend two or three weeks examining the plight of white sharecroppers at the height of the Great Depression. A documentary photographer named Walker Evans was assigned to accompany him. They were to interview and witness the hard lives of two tenant families—the Gudgers and the Ricketts—and produce an article of several thousand words. Instead, Agee stayed several months and produced a tome of nearly 500 pages, published as a book by Houghton Mifflin in 1939. Bold, passionate, accusatory, detailed to a degree I had not encountered, it is a classic piece of Americana, the single most influential book I'd ever read. It raised troubling questions about capitalism as it was practiced in America, strong on creating wealth, weak on distributing it.

Each memory I had of David tagged some quality of his character. The recollections floated up from the growing archive of our time together. Several were unforgettable. One Saturday in the late eighties David called to ask if I wanted to join him for a look at the collection of Chinese porcelains at the Headley-Whitney Museum outside Lexington. He drove to my place in Frankfort from Louisville, and we traveled the scenic Old Frankfort Pike to the museum together. The two of us probably looked pretty scruffy. He almost invariably wore old khakis and loafers, wrapping his girth in a button-down Brooks Brothers broadcloth shirt, usually a dusty blue. I wore whatever was at hand, probably jeans and a pullover or whatever shirt was closest. The museum was a handsome structure on what previously had been a horse farm flanked distantly by other horse farms, black fences extending to the blue haze of the horizon. Whoever tended the collection—a graduate student in art history, I imagine her, peering over horn-rimmed glasses—greeted us a little formally as if to say, "This isn't the mall." She asked a little officiously what she could do for us. We did not even remotely resemble the highbrows and horse people who came in designer outfits from the Garden Club to investigate the lapidary work of the museum's founder, who also had an addictive but tasteful collecting obsession. When David said we had come to see the Chinese porcelains, the young woman was taken aback a bit. She seemed less anxious, her fear of a major jewel heist being allayed somewhat though not erased. Here was someone literate enough to know the museum held an impressive run of Chinese porcelains spanning centuries and dynasties.

Not rising from her curator's desk, she directed us toward the porcelains, displays of teapots and jugs as well as the Asian version of kettles, all exhibited behind protective glass. They were beautifully shaped and glazed with intricate patterns of willows and pagodas in addition to sheer filigree. The best had not faded over the centuries though fissured with tiny age cracks. I admired them as only a tourist could. David, an avid amateur sinologist who'd read extensively about these things and the emperors who sat in marble-backed chairs in their summer palaces, studied each piece carefully and appreciatively, making mental notes about the designations of dynasty and whatever additional text turned up on the printed placards. He took it all in, extending his approval over the roll of dynasties.

When we returned to the entry area again, the curator asked—haughtily, I thought—"And how did you find our porcelains?" David nodded his approbation and added as we reached the exit door, "You might want to check a couple of the dynasty dates, especially the Tang and the Sung." The words hung in the air for a long moment. Flummoxed for having misread David, the curator performed an about-face, exuding politeness and gratitude now as she became convinced that here was one rube who knew his stuff.

David also contained a deep vein of sentiment. On the mantel in the book-filled room I call my library is a framed prose-poem that David delivered when my wife and I married in the living room of the house that I and one or two other graduate students rented on High Street in Lexington. We were married on November 30, 1972 by an Episcopalian minister who happened to live around the corner, and David, as I remember, was one of two witnesses. The prose-poem he composed as a fairy tale ended with an uncharacteristically sweet benediction:

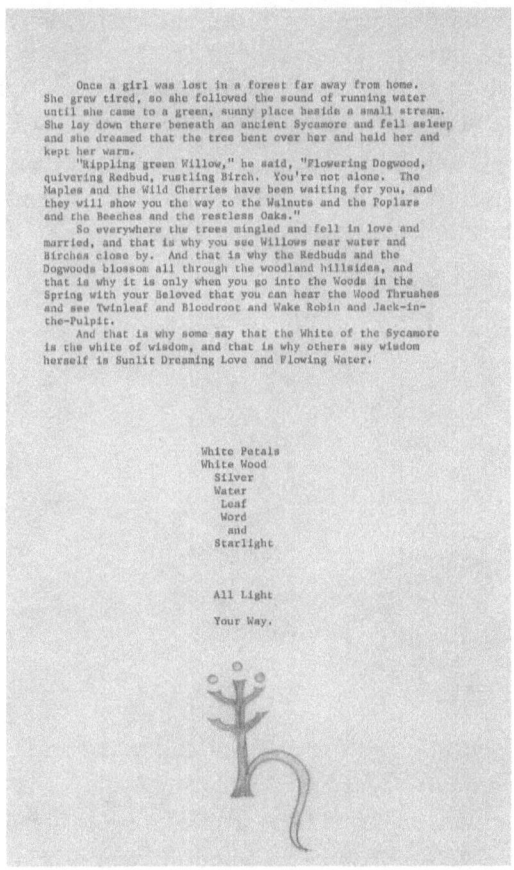

Wedding well wishes from David Orr.

Once a girl was lost in a forest far away from home. She grew tired, so she followed the sound of running water until she came to a green, sunny place beside a small stream. She lay down there beneath an ancient Sycamore and fell asleep and she dreamed that the tree bent over her and held her and kept her warm.

"Rippling green Willow," he said, "Flowering Dogwood, quivering Redbud, rustling Birch. You're not alone. The Maples and the Wild Cherries have been waiting for you, and they will show you the way to the Walnuts and the Poplars and the Beeches, and the restless Oaks."

So everywhere the trees mingled and fell in love and married, and that is why you see Willows near water and Birches close by. And that is why the Redbuds and the Dogwoods blossom all through the woodland hillsides, and that is why it is only when you go into the Woods in the Spring with your Beloved that you can hear the Wood Thrushes and see Twinleaf and Bloodroot and Wake Robin and Jack-in-the-Pulpit.

And that is why some say the White of the Sycamore is the white of wisdom, and that is why others say wisdom herself is Sunlit Dreaming Love and Flowing Water.

White Petals
White Wood
Silver
Water
Leaf
Word
and
Starlight

All Light

Your Way.

This pleasing sentiment is the case I would make that David Orr was a Parnassian with a heart, a man who not only lived in his head but in the natural world for which he had great affection, creating for his friend, for whom he had great affection, a mythological origin for diversity in nature.

In addition to our creek walking, David and I ranged farther in our re-explorations of Kentucky, searching for forgotten landscape and forgotten folkways. Memorable among these pilgrimages was our trip with David "Hunt" Wilson to Lilley's Woods, followed by an impromptu jaunt to Virginia one weekend in the mid-eighties. The three of us drove to Lilley Cornett Woods in Hunt's barely reliable Ford pickup. We wanted, as David put it, to reconstruct in our imaginations a piece of the state before it reached the state it was in—large parts of it stripped and deforested, a shadow of the magnificent wilderness Boone and the firstcomers must have experienced. We knew only that it contained some of the only old-growth forest in the Eastern United States, what we, perhaps mistakenly, called virgin forest. The tract contains 554 acres of which 252 acres are designated as old-growth, mesophytic forest—woods undisturbed by man for 150 years. According to studies, the woods are an Eden of biodiversity with 530 species of flowering plants and an estimated 700 breeding pairs of birds in addition to hosting a variety of small mammals, amphibians, and reptiles. Now under custodial control of Eastern Kentucky University, it was preserved by a feat of will of a recalcitrant owner named Lilley Cornett who steadfastly resisted efforts of local lumber agents to purchase its valuable timber. Then, we were permitted into the woods without a guide so long as we disturbed nothing and promised not to litter. Treading on what to us was sacred ground, we hiked past huge tulip poplars whose vertical shafts were not broken until lost in the thick canopy overhead. Where a tree had fallen or been struck by lightning, its trunk slowly melted into the spongey mulch in a cycle of self-enrichment. Beds of ferns rose to our waists just off the path we followed. We finally climbed to a rock shelter where we rested and lunched on steak sandwiches that Hunt's wife Jane had prepared for us—the best sandwich I've ever eaten. We talked about what we'd seen and imagined this microcosm of the past as Boone and his messmates must have witnessed it.

Somehow in our ongoing exchanges Thomas Jefferson's name came up, and we impetuously took to the road again, traveling into the toe of Virginia's foot on winding roads until we reached Jefferson's little mountain in Albemarle County. Joining one of the tours in the foyer of what David regarded as a sanctum of sanctums, we viewed the bones that the ever-curious president fetched from Big Bone Lick in northern Kentucky, one of the most important archaeological sites in eastern North America. During the tour we marveled at the president's inventiveness, not the primitive copying device by which he could keep copies of his correspondence but the dumbwaiter built into the dining room mantel just large enough to accommodate a bottle of French wine. We took it all in, noting the understory complex in which individuals held in bondage prepared and delivered his daily bread. I was especially drawn to the one-room brick dependency in which he spent a winter with his new bride while he planned construction of one of the most carefully planned domestic structures in America. I remembered the changes that were made by an amateur yet accomplished architect whose justification was that he "loved the smell of brick dust." On the way back to the parking lot David spotted a poplar seedling that he unearthed with his pocketknife, later planting it in his front yard, something associated with the American with whom he most identified. What the site authorities would regard as an act of theft we regarded as a rite of propagation, of devotion, of rescue, an homage from someone who held little else in reverence.

Though I was busy teaching elsewhere, I knew something of David's short academic career. He had graduated from University of Louisville and gone on to Northwestern University to earn a Ph.D. in Philosophy. During graduate school he and his wife Monica lived in the suburb of Evanston, which he described as an elephant graveyard—a place in the jungle where elderly elephants came to die. Somehow after completing his courses, he ran afoul of a dissertation committee on which there were sparring personalities. After some extensions and a period of habitual dilatoriness, he said the hell with it and eventually came back to Louisville, where he landed a job for six or so years teaching philosophy at U.L. on a tenure track, his academic future depending on completion of his dissertation (on what or whom I can't remember).

His reputation as a teacher was legendary. Coming at a time when college-age students were being drafted for Vietnam, he had little regard for grades, especially for those whose failing might lead to boot camp. He taught as the ancients had, peripatetically, "on the move." For one of his introductory philosophy courses, he conducted his students on campus tours to learn the species of trees growing in the green spaces that buffered classroom buildings from the factories nearby that ringed and nearly smothered the campus. He had a special reverence for the albino squirrel that led a charmed life among the walkways, fearlessly approaching students for handouts, a nervous version of the mendicant philosopher Diogenes who lounged in the dust outside a local tavern. He supplemented standard readings of Aristotle and Plato with such nonacademic guest speakers as his neighborhood fire chief and the manager of the liquor store at which he bought his wine. I once picked up a student hitchhiker who sang his praises and pronounced him cool. "He's the greatest," he affirmed. "He asked us the grades we wanted, and generally that was the grade we got." Part of my time at U.L. in law school overlapped with his. I had the habit of parking on the circle outside the law school on Friday nights, catching up on my cases before going out for a beer. On one such evening I was surprised to find a cryptic message on my windshield: "Don't let the sun set on your torts. David."

As might be anticipated, David did not secure tenure, nor did he complete his dissertation. He worked for a time as an IT specialist for a fledging computer business. During his leisure he haunted Louisville bookstores, especially the ill-fated Hawley-Cooke Booksellers and its successor, Carmichael's, started by his friend and computer work partner—the best independent bookstore in Louisville. His book expenditures did much to stabilize the finances of at least two stores. His home with its ceiling-high shelves contained books that were actually read. He also adopted several favorite restaurants, including 610 Magnolia, where he sampled wine and befriended chef and proprietor Eddie Garber. After David's death, Hunt Wilson and I were privileged to take lunch periodically at Eddie's sequestered retreat near rural Westport, where much of the conversation centered on David stories, the three of us invoking his memory and sharing his opinions on such topics as plants, food, books, ideas, and the ailing health of the planet. In addition to personal interactions with him, many of us received the mailings of his invented persona, Colonel A.P. Weng. A postcard would arrive from Weng and Associates with an arcane quote from equally arcane sources, usually something that went above my head. Once during college when I had a summer job washing dishes on Isle Royale in Lake Superior, I received a postcard addressed to "Positive Wasserman" Taylor. We took to calling him Colonel Orr. At one point, Weng and Associates sponsored a Black Athena coloring contest, each of us receiving the outline of the classical goddess. I forget the prize.

When his artist grandmother died in the late seventies, David became the administrator of what was called the Pace Trust for Community

Creative Visual Arts, a fund she set up to underwrite worthwhile arts projects. Stretching guidelines a bit, David was able to publish limited editions of several books and monographs, at least two by our mutual intellectual mentor, Guy Davenport, the English professor and polymath who directed my dissertation at University of Kentucky in the seventies. The Weng and Associates publications I own are Davenport's *Trois Caprices* (1980–81) and *Maxims of the Ancient Egyptians*. There may have been more, including one I can't locate about the adventures of a child detective. He published picture books, including a folio-size of poster art by Louisville artist Julius Friedman, best known for a Louisville Ballet promotion in which a ballet dancer's arched foot is balanced on an upturned egg. Another was Guy Davenport's translation of Antisthenes (445 BC–365 BC), a disciple of Socrates who rivaled Diogenes for the distinction of being the founder of the Cynic school of philosophy: "Plato is a wienie." *Cynic* derives from the tradition that Antisthenes "barked" at the follies and injustices of society, *cynic* meaning doglike. David's own outlook was sometimes colored by Oscar Wilde's famous definition of cynic—someone who knows the price of everything and the value of nothing.

Living in Frankfort, I had only occasional contact with my best friend. This was before the widespread use of what we called "celery" phones and texting. Sometimes he came to Frankfort, always I visited him in Louisville at Christmas. His daughter Laura, to whom I gave the egg after his passing, was my godchild, and his family and mine convened each Christmas, catching up and exchanging small gifts, usually books. He witnessed my sons growing up and kidded Julia, their younger sister. During the summer months he encouraged us to visit his backyard pool. He offered advice on my writing and often referred to me as P.R. Taylor, short for "Porch Rail." He thought I was too busy and needed to relax. He once told me, only half facetiously, that he did not believe a gentleman should conduct business before noon. Our lives diverged though we met when I came to Louisville or when he made it to the capital, coming out of the provinces, as I jokingly referred to the largest city in the Commonwealth.

David Orr, dying way too young, was an American original. He suffered the complexities of being an American who looked beyond what was before him, of thinking deeply about the world and his place in it. There was a portion of him that was haunted, a morbid side, reflected in his humor that tended toward darkness. Once in his cups at a party he became blood brother with an intellectual counterpart with whom he opened his arm with a "church key," a piece of triangular metal used to open beer cans. He never seemed fully at home with his gifts of insight and intelligence, never fully satisfied with himself. An eagle aloft has many options. He was like the boulder Aristotle described that contained a form whose release by mallet and chisel would produce a sculpture. What to commit to? A year younger, a century wiser than most of us, David dwelled in realms that were not always bridgeable. Before he left for California with the sycamore egg, he prophetically told one of our mutual friends that he wouldn't be coming back. I've pondered this ambiguous pronouncement for years. As teenagers we had a steady diet of folk-singer Pete Seeger, among whose offerings was a song with the lyric we both admired: "I don't want to get adjusted to this world. I've got a home that's so much greater, I'm going to go to sooner or later. I don't want to get adjusted to this world."

Though David probably didn't hold much credence in the existence of a next world, being adjusted was not one of his existential goals. Registering his dissatisfaction with adjustment, which to him was another name for complacency, his legacy is a large composite of many small leavings. In one of his Weng cards, he composed what masqueraded as an excerpt from a treatise on antiquity, as if copied by some classicist or mythical scholar of the ancient world. Read and remembered over 60 years ago, I can only approximate the contents of what comes across as a prayer or admonition: "Please, this is a house sacred to Mother Dindymene, sacred to the muses. Let other men leave their metaphors at the door. Things are not as they say they are."

These words come to mind when I read a poem that doesn't ring true or one whose images are lame or too exhausted to breathe. Dindymene turns out to be a surname of Cybele, an Anatolian goddess of Phrygia, the principal goddess whose cult was spread across mainland Greece by Greek colonists living in Asia Minor. The Romans converted her into Magna Mater, the "Great Mother," a proto earth mother like Gaia. David's mind was full of cosmic texts, the overflow from an overactive imagination and an effort to discover sources whose origins might provide answers to life's persistent questions.

At his memorial, held at the old U.L. School of Music bordering Cherokee Park on Alta Vista Road in Louisville, both Wendell Berry and

Guy Davenport, two of David's correspondents and daimons, delivered eulogies. Somewhere I have a manuscript of his poems, one of which contained a line from Ezra Pound's *Cantos*: "Grass is nowhere out of place." I see David's exuberance and generosity in the gaudy plywood rooster he bestowed on me and now perches atop a corner cupboard in my living room, the whimsical creation of Louisville folk artist Marvin Finn. I recall his odd mannerism of cocking his head and modestly gazing at his feet as if to see if they were still intact. I also can see the cowlick over his forehead that he unconsciously swept back to set his hair in place. I remember David in his 1976 Christmas gift to me of *Jefferson's Nephews*, the account of a murder performed in western Kentucky by two of his idol's nephews—one of the best books I know to understand the hardships of settlement in frontier Kentucky. I honor him in his suggestion that I read James Agee whose message, especially now, screams for compassion and social justice. I remember him in his received opinions, his slightly skewed outlook, and for his insatiable appetite for learning that boosted my own first forays into serious reading and creative writing. He was my pre-Google encyclopedia, my indulgent instructor whose spiritual paternity cannot be denied even after the last postcard he addressed to me prophetically and unforgettably, its imagined arriving received on the banks of a remote fjord in rural Denmark: "The egg and I have gone West."

In the Matter of Reuben

When I was eight or nine, for the first time I can remember, my father took me to the spring at Worthington in the farming neighborhood where he had lived as a child and where our family had farmed for five generations. After his father, an inveterate tobacco chewer, died of cancer, his mother moved her young family to Louisville, leaving what was then farmland in eastern Jefferson County for life in the city. The spring, known locally as Shop Spring, still forms a dark pool beneath a clump of trees at a corner where Chamberlain Lane, bordered by pasture and cultivated fields, makes a sharp turn an eighth mile or so from the site that was my father's first home, just at the point where Wolf Pen Branch Road t-intersected with Chamberlain Lane. The spring was a local landmark, dating from settlement times when land seekers vied for acreage with a reliable source of water. Life-giving water from an invisible aquifer welled up through a dark cavity to become Shop Spring Branch, a feeder stream that still trickles down flags of limestone to a larger tributary emptying into Harrods Creek about eight miles northeast of Louisville. My father remarked that it was a never-failing spring even as streams and branches around it dried up during times of drought. Always there was a long-handled metal dipper that hung from a nail tacked into an overshadowing maple tree. It was a quiet place, a refuge from the sunny fields, where we dipped into a clear pool of reliable water from a hidden source.

I can remember his identifying the small insects whose hairlike shadows twitched along the creek bottom as water striders. He told me that since he was my age he had dipped the cup into the dark pool on a hot day for a refreshing swig, a ritual, warm weather or cold, he had probably followed all of his life. Dunking that communal cup and swallowing, he would dip it again and offer it to me. The water was cooler than the air about us and had a slightly tinny taste. Beyond it were sunny fields that had fed his and a dozen other families since the wilderness of lower Harrods Creek was felled generations ago, the woodlands transformed to cropland of wheat and corn and potatoes whose bounty had held a small and intricately connected farming community together. We would never stay long as he then went about some errand or another, sometimes delivering legal papers to one of his clients or asking permission to pick blackberries in a favored patch. Whatever the destination, my father would climb into his Willys jeep, I would fasten the canvas seatbelt, and we were gone. For me, a city boy in the country, it was an adventure. For him, it must have been a bittersweet revisiting of his past. Though he had quit the country most of a lifetime ago, he had left his heart.

Only later when we gathered watercress one summer day above the spring did I recognize that the pond, located just above it on higher ground fifty or sixty yards away, was a kind of reservoir, a holding basin for the never-ending waters from somewhere in the dark of the earth. In the midst of change, it was a constant. Along its banks we pulled watercress to add to my mother's summer salads. Its stringy roots had a pungent, earthy smell that carried the musk of some eternal fecundity. Placing it in a bucket, my father brought it back to the city as a trophy to spice up the table for the sharp taste of wild greens not sold at Winn-Dixie. The pond was full of frogs that bellowed in the spring and plopped into loops of algae when we violated their mucky border world. Off from it maybe another forty yards was an ordinary two-story clapboard farmhouse surrounded by tall shade trees. The simple yet dignified form of the house had the unspoken authority of age and permanence.

"That's a Taylor house over there," my father said offhandedly, pointing at it over the ridge. "Under those clapboards you see are logs, and in the field yonder is a Taylor graveyard." He gestured vaguely over the fields toward a distant tree line. He gave no more details, and I wrongly assumed that was all he knew. It wasn't by a long shot.

The farmhouse perched on a little knoll among a few lofty shade trees, surrounded by fields whose fence lines were bordered with more trees. From childhood he had known the man whose family until recently had lived in the house, Doug Littrell, a captain in the state police. Which Taylor had once lived there he never told me, maybe because he didn't know or maybe, less likely, didn't think it important. More than once he mentioned the graveyard somewhere behind the house where several generations of Taylors and Chamberlains—their neighbors and friends— had been laid to rest after active lives in this tight-knit farming community.

Most of his childhood neighbors were farmers, though the Chamberlains for years had also run a blacksmith shop where horses were shod, tools sharpened on a foot-powered grinding wheel, and machinery refitted or repaired. Which is how the spring got its name. Shop Spring—from the original shop resembling nothing so much as a barn—in 1869 was relocated at the end of Chamberlain Lane where it intersected with old Brownsboro Road, U.S. 22. There remains a barn on the site of the original Shop Spring but no sign of a house. Perhaps, like my father's first home, it had burned and been reabsorbed into woodland pasture. My father was the last Taylor to live on family ground where his ancestors had settled after the Revolutionary War, the last in a farming family that also produced a physician or two and, at least briefly, a state legislator. I knew that his father, Charles Oscar, had chosen farming as his livelihood, something by all accounts he loved. He had raised tobacco on a large scale. In addition to planting his own land, he leased acreage in adjacent counties. My father, Joe Howard (never Joseph), had been born in 1905 near Sligo in Henry County where Oscar, as he was known, had leased tobacco ground. My Uncle Orin or maybe my father had told me that Oscar had died relatively young from cancer of the jaw. Uncle Orin once mentioned that a picture of his cancer-ridden jaw appeared in a medical textbook. Only later did I light on the irony that what killed him—his chewing of tobacco—had also been his livelihood.

Charles Oscar Taylor, tobacco farmer, author's grandfather.

I had been told as a child that the first Taylor in what became a kind of neighborhood enclave of Taylors had immigrated from Orange County in north-central Virginia and was an officer in the Revolution, a captain named Reuben Taylor. That was all I knew about the first Worthington Taylors though the gaps in family history have occupied my imagination for over 60 years. What brought him to Virginia's westernmost county after the war I did not learn until years later when my curiosity about family—at least my father's side of it— steered me to genealogical sources.

Through a Taylor matriarch I met in Lexington—a grand scholar of all things Taylor—I laid my hands on Mary Taylor Brewer's *From Log Cabins to the White House: A History of the Taylor Family*, a 1985 compendium of the Virginia branches of the Taylors, long out of print. From it I learned that Reuben was one of twelve sons of Col. George Francis Taylor's two marriages, the first to Rachel Gibson, the second to Sarah Taliaferro Conway, widow of a Capt. Francis Conway, and daughter of Col. John Taliaferro. I learned that in 1761 his first wife, Rachel, became infected from smallpox after insisting on nursing her son, George Jr., who had contracted the disease during his service in the French and Indian War. Both died. In 1767, George, Sr. soon married Sarah Taliaferro Conway. They had one son, George Conway Taylor, who was born in 1769. When war broke out, George Conway Taylor was too young to enlist, but the other ten sons served in various services and regiments, all of them, it was said, officers. Col. George Taylor (1711–1792), in addition to being a grand progenitor, a kind of Virginia Priam, was a politician/farmer, holding a seat in Virginia's House of Burgesses. In the years preceding the Revolution he organized and drilled the Orange County Militia, was a member of the Committee of Safety in 1774, as well as the Virginia Convention in 1775. He had fought in the French and Indian War, was elected repeatedly as the Clerk of Orange County, serving 23 years from 1750 to 1772 when his son James succeeded him. By the time of the outbreak of war he was sixty-five, too old to enlist. Instead, he must have encouraged his sons, who likely needed little encouragement.

Details about the early Taylors reminded me of the flitting shadows of the water striders. They were a presence, but it was difficult to see where they were going, where they had been. They lacked faces. So far as I know, there is no likeness of Reuben that survives, no picture of the young captain resplendent in the distinctive uniform of the Second Canadian

Regiment, a form-fitting cutaway coat, a cross sash and a vest of many buttons, a high-crowned hat shaped like a window in a Gothic church. Maybe a ceremonial sword. Nor an image of a flush-faced old man stiff in a dark formal burial and church coat he never otherwise wore, posed before the fire in winter to ease his arthritis. Other than a few expressions attributed to him, I do not have a word Reuben said except for the will composed with the help of legal forms or a country lawyer to distribute his worldly goods to his heirs.

Reuben's image was never arrested in light because he died in 1824, fifteen years before photography was invented. Some of his kin—his nephew Edmund Haynes Taylor, Jr., for example—had their faces memorialized in oil by such professionals as Matthew Harris Jouett or a handful of other portraitists active in central Kentucky and Louisville. Given the time and technology lag between the Old World and the New, photographs were not common until his children's and their children's generation. Though there are a few silhouettes and sketches as well as a few portraits surviving of his forebears, his was a farming family on the frontier, one given to sharpening plows and anticipating the weather rather than decorating the mantel or addressing posterity. Though one of his sons became a physician, the one from whom I descend, no medical charts survive him giving his medical history and vital statistics. I imagine him looking much like my father—a wiry man a little below average height, a narrow head and prominent nose, strong but not robust, a little given to a soft middle in old age. What his voice sounded like is of course unknowable, heard only by those four or five generations gone.

Necessarily, the portrait I try to reconstruct of him has its vacancies. I start by assembling shards like fragments of a ceramic pot from antiquity from which the whole can at least partially be glued into a form with some pieces still missing. Initially, these shards materialize from brief references in the writings or recollections of others.

What caught my notice in the few sources at hand was that Capt. Reuben Taylor received 4,000 acres of land for his services during the Revolution. I naturally assumed that Reuben, one of the younger brothers—born in 1757—came to Kentucky after the war in order to make a life for himself and whatever family he had, or would have, on 4,000 acres of land situated in the Worthington area. What had happened to it? Did he gamble or sell it away? Uncle Orin had once commented that Reuben's grandson, Philip Richard Taylor, periodically sold off land to keep himself afloat, but 4,000 acres? How had square miles of land in what would become the state's most populous county near Kentucky's largest city dissipated into several hundred acres. Where was it now? These questions nagged me. Beyond ordinary curiosity about my forbears, they drove me to seek answers.

For those answers I turned first to Uncle Orin, my father's elder brother, who lived across the street from us in Louisville in the house his mother, my grandmother, bought in the Crescent Hill neighborhood of Louisville when his father died in 1916. In the late sixties, he was the oldest living member of my close family and presumably the one who had the longest memory, drawn from the reservoir of happenings that were his life. While living on Pleasantview, my father met his future wife, my mother, Dorothy Dey, who lived directly across the street. She was eight years younger, a bobbysoxer when he was in college. He wooed her on the motorcycle his indulgent mother permitted him to own.

Philip Richard Taylor, author's father's grandfather, as a young man, about 1860.

Though my father never spoke of it, relations between him and his brother were strained. They did not visit each other and seldom spoke though they lived across the street from each other for years. I later learned that my father felt that after his marriage, Orin, still living with his mother, whose name was Minnie Nuckols Taylor but was simply called "Ma'am," had neglected their mother. This was the apparent source of the friction, though Orin, older by seven or eight years, apparently felt that my father, the youngest of Minnie's four children, had been treated as the fair-haired child, being sent to military school and on to college while he, born in 1897, reached adulthood just at the time of World War I and enlisted at Camp Zachary Taylor near Louisville, returning from Europe to work in a pet store, a business he later owned. Though resentment between the brothers must have simmered just below the surface, whatever ill feelings there were did not extend to my brother and me.

So on holidays at Thanksgiving, Easter, and Christmas when my brother Douglas and I would return from the University of Kentucky, we climbed the steps to the modest bungalow where Orin lived with his wife, Anna Mabel, and quizzed him about Worthington and the Taylors. Wearing khakis and invariably dressed from fall until spring in a Pendleton plaid shirt, Orin always seemed pleased to see us and take our questions though by nature he was serious and a little reserved. A veteran of World War I, he was especially tight-lipped about his experiences in western Europe. On one visit he fetched the Italian dagger that his uncle, Dr. Philip Richard Taylor, Jr. (P.R.), gave him (and he later gave me) before he embarked on the troop ship that bore him and his comrades overseas. Thin and finely balanced in its metal scabbard, the knife was carried by twenty-year-old Orin in his leggings during his tour of duty in France. Whether he used the dagger in defense of himself and his country is doubtful and ultimately unknowable since he was close-mouthed about his experiences. The plain economy of his clothing and reserved manner were reflected in what he would share with us, though occasionally he would drop the wall of reserve and open up.

With rare candor he later confided to us how he came by the knife. It seems P.R., a physician, was a ladies' man. One of his lady friends, he told us, was married to a burly fellow who would be more than a match for P.R. physically, so he bought the dagger to even his chances. When Orin enlisted, P.R. passed it on to his nephew, having no children of his own. And Orin passed it on to me. The only photograph I have of P.R. has a sepia tone and presents a behatted gent with an imperial goatee standing proudly in his hunting jacket, a brace of inverted pheasants in one hand, a shotgun cradled under his arm. For some reason he seems puffed up with more than a hunter's pride. Oddly, the hat and the beard, the benign eyes brought to mind photographs I'd seen of Robert E. Lee.

Dr. Philip Richard Taylor, Jr., brother of the author's grandfather.

On another occasion Orin told us a story that would be easy to disbelieve had there been a reason to lie about it. It concerned a pocket watch that according to family tradition had been bestowed on one of the Taylors by no less a personage than General Washington. Why or what the occasion was I don't know, though as there were ten Taylor brothers who served as officers under him in the defense of Virginia and the struggle for independence, it is very likely that Washington knew some of them. While Orin was off in Europe, he said that "the kids"— meaning his two younger sisters and my father, who was the youngest sibling—had removed it from wherever it was kept, played with it, and somehow broken it. Why someone did not set the pieces aside for safekeeping or possible repair he did not say. Nor did Orin mention what came of it, though it's possible the pieces were consumed in the fire that destroyed their home shortly after the war. I can remember my father pointing out the house site on Chamberlain Lane across the road from the intersection with Wolf Pen Brach Road. All that remained was a little swale in a pasture with a few old trees marking what must have been the yard he played in. I took in this tale with a little skepticism at first, but Orin was a sober, even somber, man not given to lying.

The final answer to where the land went did not come until a year or so ago through my son Willis, whose curiosity and research skills took him to official legal records, indicating that the 4,000 acres were not located in Kentucky but in Ohio. As further surprise, the land was not granted until 1798, and it did not come from Virginia, but from the federal government: four 1,000-acre grants signed by President John Adams. By that time Reuben was planning to settle with a young family in Worthington, invested in one place with family and new friends, understandably reluctant to move again. I surmise that he must have sold the granted land and applied the proceeds to improve and possibly enlarge his holdings at Worthington. That was one mystery explained.

I continued to pick up specifics about Reuben's life in dibs and dabs, scouring the indexes of every book I suspected might contain a reference to him. I also mined the plentiful sources on-line. Because he was neither a president nor a general (one of his cousins was, another both), I seldom found more than a few sentences, most of them relating to his service during the war as one of ten brothers who took up arms in the rebellion.

Ten or so years ago, a kind individual I didn't know left a note and a phone number at the bookstore I co-own, asking if I'd read Russell Chamberlain's *The Early Harrods Creek Settlements and the Kentucky Branch of the Chamberlain Family*, an unpublished family genealogy. I hadn't, and this gentleman agreed to let me photocopy it as he stood by, afraid to lose what I came to see as a treasure of information about my family's past. Years after Russell Chamberlain's death, I found a copy on my own, a spiral-ringed typescript of 403 pages that has proven to be a gold mine of Chamberlain and Taylor lore as well as an informal history of the Worthington neighborhood from settlement times to the mid-20th century.

Though I don't remember meeting Russell Chamberlain as a child, I have a vivid recollection of encountering Russell's brother Carl, a blacksmith whose shop was a large barn at the corner of Chamberlain Lane and Brownsboro Road across from a Worthington cemetery where the Nuckolses, my maternal grandmother's parents, rested and where my father and others had come to cut weeds and mow among the headstones. Even then, I sensed that the shop was special, a throwback to an earlier, simpler time. Carl was a burly, no-nonsense man who could improvise miracles in repairing farm implements, forging unobtainable parts, or welding equipment to join what had been sundered. I remember him with goggles presiding over huge canisters of gas hooked up to his welding apparatus. He wore a striped railroad cap, the bill reversed on his head, a man with swollen forearms of a thickness that bespoke an intimacy with the hammer. I later learned that he was expert with furnaces and raced motorcycles, it was said for a time performing in a circus. The shop must also have been a center of local news and gossip, mostly male gossip about hunting and fish catches, farm prices, or local mishaps, a place where off-color jokes were told and retold.

The shop itself was housed in a gray-sided barn that contained a small furnace, a forge, and a huge anvil. It smelled of machine oil and rust and had a spotted bucket for chewers to dispel their excess tobacco juice. Its interior was crammed with metal parts, dusty implements, and whatever Carl happened to be working on for his neighbor: parts of a harrow or a broken plough, his workbench covered with orphaned pieces of iron and bushels of screws and bolts. Plough points and mowing blades were sharpened, and wagons and farm sleds were custom-built there. I had the notion, then as now, that Carl Chamberlain could make or fix anything. Russell, his brother, was the scholar, interested in collecting stories and the larger patterns of local events.

According to Russell Chamberlain in his rich history, the Chamberlains and Taylors had a long association as neighbors and friends. As early as 1829, Taylors had helped Jacob Chamberlain build the original blacksmith shop at Shop Spring on the northern bend of the military road that became Chamberlain Lane, an enterprise that benefited the neighborhood, cutting down on trips to town for parts or repairs, giving it, in addition to the later Worthington store and church, a place to exchange stories and simply pass the time. Their families had intermarried. Taylors and Chamberlains lie buried in the same family cemetery nearby, the one my father had mentioned and which I had tried to reimagine. Nearly fifty years ago, I met Russell, then maybe in his early seventies, when he served as volunteer curator of a nonprofit history museum in downtown Louisville. The collection was housed in a rundown building near the main public library between 3rd and 4th Streets. An oversized jar for donations stood by the door. Inside was a genial retiree who brimmed with enthusiasm and tidbits of local knowledge. Aflame with history, he gave me a tour of the museum at a time when the closest thing Louisville had to a history museum was the Filson Club (now called the Filson Historical Society), which functioned mostly as a research library for Kentucky history, its shelves crammed with books, its walls covered with portraits of august patriarchs and a few, very few, nineteenth-century women.

Among this accumulation of relics and oddments were natural curiosities and fossils from the coral beds at the Falls of the Ohio as well as a few artifacts from Louisville's beginnings: pot shards, bone buttons, rusty utensils, bits of thick, green bottle glass, and fragments of rusted metal rescued from building sites and middens near the Ohio River. In an un-Faulknerian sense, Russell Chamberlain was an individual consumed by the past. Unlike many amateur historians, he was a diligent pursuer of facts, insistent on getting details right.

Only later did I discover his passion to create a record of his family and the place they inhabited, a place that even forty years ago was in flux. Worthington's broad potato-producing fields were being subdivided into suburban developments with rustic and euphoric names that gave only a grudging nod to its colorful and sometimes violent past. Some of the roads were named for those who lived along them—Chamberlain, Barbour, Dorsey, and Simcoe, for example. Here I should mention that my father secured me my first job, culling and bagging potatoes that local farmers had brought in from the fields. Sixteen, I was paid a dollar an hour and was impressed with the hard work of local farmers who brought in truckloads of potatoes with mountainous pride. Russell must have had a capacious memory that stemmed from his passion to know who his people were and how they had got on in the world. He became their chronicler. I've often wished I had the questions for him then that I have now, for his book contained many stories about my family I would never have otherwise encountered. He must have spent much of his time foraging his memory and seeking out stories from local old-timers. His perspective and attention to seemingly insignificant details fleshed out contexts and clarified many of my questions that dangled from family stories like unfinished sentences.

One such story about Reuben—a near brush with death from an Indian—read like something out of a dime novel but with just enough deviation from typical plot outcomes to make it credible. Sometime after 1799 when the veteran and his family moved permanently to the log house he had constructed across from Shop Spring, Reuben—getting up in years according to Chamberlain's account—one sultry summer afternoon was hoeing weeds in his cornfield within sight of his home. His dog went with him. What breed it was we are not told but probably a fyce or hunting hound that doubled as a pet. This dog accompanied Reuben to the field and began barking. The cause of the commotion was a single Indian lurking in the nearby woods. When at last the barking drew Reuben's notice, he spotted the Indian closing the distance in a menacing way. Startled, he threw down his hoe and struck out for the house, where he'd left his rifle. Gaining in his pursuit of the shambling old man, the younger finally hurled his tomahawk. It struck Reuben in the back but fortunately with the blunt handle end instead of the sharpened head. It stunned him momentarily, and he went down, causing only a deep bruise but with enough force to stop the desperate fugitive, at least momentarily. The pursuer, apparently without a rifle of his own, then drew a hunting knife to kill his prey when the dog, loyal to his master, jumped him from behind, biting him on the legs, distracting him and costing time as the surprised assailant stopped to kick at the dog with its bared teeth and menacing yelps. When Reuben reached the house a few yards ahead of his pursuer, the younger man gave up the chase and fled into the forest before Reuben could fetch his rifle. Someone speculated plausibly that the young brave was out to prove his mettle as a ritual to entering manhood.

Later, when Reuben told the story to his neighbor Thomas Grant, he is said to have said, "Tom, if that Indian had lifted my scalp, he would have had a great disappointment, 'cause he wouldn't have got enough hair for a fly switch." Those reported words are the only quoted speech I've found of Capt. Reuben Taylor, who regarded his near death with the self-deprecating humor characteristic of the rural South.

From available sources I knew that Reuben Taylor was born January 10, 1757, the tenth son of George and Rachel Moore Taylor at Rapidan, Orange County, Virginia, at a time when it took large families to tend to large unmechanized farms. Rapidan, located on both sides of the Rapidan River that divides Orange and Culpeper counties, was and is a small rural community five miles northeast of the town of Orange. Orange was not unlike Worthington, the rural community in Jefferson County where Reuben would eventually settle and die on November 30, 1824, a farmer and veteran of the American Revolution.

One of the central inconsistencies of Reuben's life is that he, along with his family who invested themselves so much in the Revolution and were ardent advocates of individual freedom, were slaveholders. In the adjacent Albemarle County dwelt the author of the Declaration of Independence who engaged in similar self-deception, capable of writing and believing that "all men are created equal" but content to own other human beings though his conscience pricked occasionally in his writings and also must have rankled in his daily life. There is no defense to this position then or today, though the Taylors and many of their neighbors were unquestioning inheritors of custom, an established norm in Virginia since 1619—then over 150 years. Wrong though it was, it was the system on which the agrarian economy rested, and few seemed to contest it so long as it benefited them. There is little evidence that Reuben and the class of slaveholders who profited from the cruel institution troubled their consciences. They relied on convenient theories about inferiority and a necessary dependence of those that served them, the owners themselves propagating and reinforcing the practice when they could.

My windfall glimpse into Reuben's life came as revelation through Willis's digging that the house I had known as "a Taylor cabin" was "the Taylor cabin": Reuben's. The house that Reuben and his family had lived in I assumed was long gone—torn down, burned, or demolished by neglect. I assumed the house my father had pointed out had belonged to another Taylor. Here it was by Shop Spring, intact and still standing, having lasted over 220 years. Months passed before we could arrange to see it. We repeatedly attempted to gain admittance, slowed by the tenant's understandable temporizing. *Who were these strangers*, he must have asked himself, *who wants to root around my house?* Unwilling to let go, Willis pestered from time to time, and finally the tenant agreed to let us visit as he was moving out.

The appointed day to see Reuben Taylor's log house was March 22, 2019, a crisp spring day, breezy and temperate. I drove with my friend Patrick Kennedy from Frankfort to Worthington to meet Willis and explore for the first time the inside of the log house my ancestor built and lived in over 200 years ago, the house where his descendants had lived until the early decades of the 20th century. It stood like a resilient dinosaur among the upscale residences that were creeping toward what remained of the fields and hollows whose dimensions had shrunk dramatically to a ghost of the woodlands and expanses of early settlement.

Patrick, my close friend who'd recently retired from the Kentucky Heritage Council and had inspected many such structures over his career, came partly out of curiosity but mostly as a favor to me. He had explored old buildings and diagnosed their ailments. He had also lived in a cabin he rebuilt and had mastered the hand skills necessary to build such a structure, applying the limited technology with which it had been originally constructed. He was an avid collector of period tools—broad axes, adzes, mauls, draw knives, and simple plumb bobs. With a froe he had riven shakes from chunks of white oak to recreate period roofs. He would have fit in well with frontier craftsmen, having worked on such historic structures as Mount Vernon and at least one cabin in the new African American Museum in Washington, D.C.

Arriving at the appointed time, the former tenant agreed to let us see the interior of the rented farmhouse though he was busy loading his possessions. From the outside the house itself was not all that much to look at. Never a showplace, it was a standard two-story clapboard box with a small porch sheltered by a shed roof and an ell with additional rooms, a modest structure resembling dozens built during the past 150 years in the Worthington neighborhood. Most of its sisters had burned, been torn down for roads or subdivisions, or been modernized beyond recognition to accommodate the conventions of life in the Louisville suburbs 200 years later.

Double pen dogtrot cabin of Capt. Reuben Taylor, built before 1800.

The house must have originally stood in a clearing in the wilderness, some of which was winnowed out to build it. The house—more than a simple settlement cabin—must have been larger than most of its few neighbors. Now it was dwarfed among ranks of brick dwellings along paved streets studded with lampposts, another wave of settlement, this one swift and tidal. It was part of what was becoming a small city.

An old pickup was backed to the edge of the porch and a portly man, sixtyish and wearing a baseball cap, gestured us in as he continued loading. We introduced ourselves and shook hands.

"You're welcome to look all you like," he said good-naturedly, displaying that exaggerated politeness natural to rural Kentuckians, a carryover, I suspected, from frontier days when strangers were genuinely welcomed. We offered to help but he said no, he could do it himself.

We entered a narrow hall that ran between the two downstairs rooms. We could not decide whether the wide-planked floors were ash or maybe poplar or both. The ceilings were low, and a narrow stairway with an elegantly simple handrail rose up one wall. Practicality overruled grandeur. Both walls and handrail appeared to be original, and I imagined Reuben, older by then, laboring up the stairs to bed, the lips of each tread rounded by his passings.

The first things I noticed in the room to the right off the front hall were the fins of a modern ceiling fan. The outside wall, windowless, had a rebuilt modern brick hearth that was totally incongruent with the original exposed logs. They were of a width found only in old- growth chestnut and poplar trees, each log separated by a white band of chinking that seemed intact.

Everywhere I felt the presence of my ancestors. Though I could not replay all the dramas, great and small, that had taken place within these log walls, I could imagine Reuben and his wife Rebecca in the evenings sitting by firelight in Lincolnesque repose after a day's labors, Rebecca having performed her domestic chores, tending the younger children, and preparing meals while Reuben worked somewhere in the fields outside, returning at noon and at suppertime.

Much of the original fabric of the house remained intact. To get a better sense of just how much, Patrick and I climbed the narrow stairs to duplicate rooms on either side of the hall and an even narrower set of stairs going to the attic, or loft, probably used for storage or possibly for additional sleeping space for children. There we found a simple but serviceable door with hand-forged hinges. The house was stable. The siding was hand-planed and beaded, attached to the building with "wrought square shank, rose-head nails," as Patrick described them. Despite superficial alterations we were gazing on a two-story, double pen cabin with a breezeway or "dogtrot" between the two pens, built sometime toward the end of the eighteenth century.

I stood by, still in wonderment at penetrating a time warp to visit my ancestor in his former dwelling. I felt no ominous presences, no ghosts, no whoopings of banshees or wails of sickly children. Over everything there was a sense of repose, a heavy silence. In the first stage of construction the cabin was probably a single-room structure with notched logs, a stone chimney, and narrow stairs leading to the gabled space upstairs where he and others probably slept.

We climbed to the loft. Patrick inspected the dimly lit room whose only illumination came from a small window, probably original, at either end of the gable. He pointed out that the inside wall of the room on the left side of the house still had clapboard, indicating that the house had been added on to from an original single pen because it had once been an outside door before a dogtrot and second pen was later added, probably to accommodate a growing family. The hand-planed siding had a bead, a long ornamental fissure that ran its length, indicating that it was very early. Considering it, I imagined the house evolving from a place of shelter and defense, preliminary and fairly crude, into a home, simple but adequate, built sufficiently well to last over 220 years and counting. Going outside, we found that the entire house had been set on a drystone foundation—one of the reasons for its longevity. The clapboards were probably old growth poplar, its blond wood known for its durability and imperviousness to insects. Except for the two in the attic, all of the windows had been replaced circa 1900, probably after 1907 when Reuben's descendants sold it out of the family.

We took a few more photos and left, still excited but also a little somber about the passage of time. The house seemed rooted to its place by long habit, a witness to the recent changes about it as the land was converted from agricultural to residential uses.

Reuben died at age sixty-seven, December 16, 1824, of no cause I've been able to discover other than old age and an incredibly active life. His last will held no surprises. His wife survived him, and he left her a life interest in the house and farm. His children would ultimately inherit the property. If my math is right and there is no other real estate, Reuben owned approximately 700 acres in the area at the time of his death, a considerable amount of land, which was the principal asset of his estate. Like many Kentuckians, he was land rich and cash poor.

Research, like measuring the flow of water, is an imprecise science. And Time is a Nile, wide and long and deep. We seine it with a puny net, its mesh sometimes harvesting a spangled catch but as often turning up nothing but minnows and throwbacks. Much that is golden slips through. Questions we ache to have answered find no archive beyond the circuit clerk's office and raw columns of census statistics. Connecting the dots often depends on happy accidents and blind luck, a few fortunate stumblings—sometimes an unsummoned impulse to check the index of a remotely related book or uncovering a bonanza in some unpromising footnote, a researcher's joy.

At times I believed I could feel Reuben as a witness to his own story, breathing over my shoulder and trying to tell me things, to set me on the right path when I deviated from the truth of his life as he knew and understood it. He ignited an impulse to question a point or infer a result or to make a leap spanning gaps in the trail he inadvertently left us to follow. I often consulted him in my imagination, asking the trite and perennial question, *what would Reuben do, why did Reuben do this, do that.* And sometimes he would tell me. However he directed this narrative, it was clear that I was a guest in his house, that I would not be conducted to the inner rooms of his past where even those who knew him closest seldom entered. Guests, even those united with him by blood, were kept to the parlor, never taken upstairs.

Much I will never know. Reuben had vanished like smoke up the chimney of blackened stones. The logs have soaked up the voices in that house, the smells as well as its belongings. If the bodies that inhabited these rooms are gone, what remains are the bones of their lives. What we know of his fleshy self we decrypt now from paper or cyberspace. His descendants have stepped away from home ground. Reuben's house, absent the lives that knew it as no others, is a relic, a chance survivor. The doors of his past are now secured with invisible locks to which there is no magic skeleton key.

What were Reuben Taylor's routines, the tone of his voice, his habits and idiosyncrasies, his favorite color, the tics in his speech? Did he play a musical instrument or sing? Was he religious in more than a conventional sense? What was the nature of his intellectual life? Was he quick of temper? Was he haunted by the experience of war or a single warrior bent on snuffing out the life of an intruder? Was he a loving father and husband? Had he phobias? Did he suffer from dementia in old age? Did he try to replicate the patterns of social life he had known in Virginia? Did he grieve for his lost brothers? Did he know despair as he came to terms with his mortality? History, even with famous personages, seldom records these things because history is seldom intimate—once the pawn of paper and now to databases. History can never recapture the lived present, the pulse of the experience as it happens. It works in the past tense. So we attempt ourselves to clothe the bones. The log house my son and I visited stands on shaky ground, its future uncertain. At Shop Spring we stop to sip water from a spring whose waters braid and flow to the Gulf of Mexico. The cup is gone from the tree. None of us is more permanent than heel prints in the mud. We follow where they lead us.

My Civil War Education

Growing up in Louisville during the 1950s, I often heard that Kentucky had waited until the Civil War ended before seceding, as though its citizens had the benefit of watching a horse race and then the privilege of betting on the loser. I could not, beyond some vague notions of romance and contagious veneration of the Lost Cause, understand why. Was it because of our collective sympathy for the underdog or the mythologizing of the agrarian South by writers like Thomas Nelson Page and Margaret Mitchell whose work was part of the regional sanctification of the Confederacy after its demise? When I was old enough to start asking whether Kentucky's switching of loyalties was true and, if so, why, I settled first on the knowledge that Kentucky during the war had remained in federal hands and that most Kentuckians were loyal to the Union though regarding itself, and regarded by others both North and South, as Southern in its sentiments and allegiances, which included an economy that had slavery near its heart. Though Kentucky's agriculture did not rely on great numbers of forced laborers, the exploitation of African Americans in Kentucky had been a tradition since its earliest settlement. The state had a total of 225,483 slaves in the 1860 census or 19 percent of its total population, making it ninth among the fifteen slaveholding states. The Bluegrass and Lexington as well as western Kentucky held large numbers of enslaved persons. Louisville itself was an anomaly, the state's center of commerce and manufacturing. A railhead and major supply center for the Union Army, it was one of the only Southern cities actually to prosper during the war.

As a teenager, I had read about Appomattox and Gettysburg as well as biographies of Grant and Lee and other facets of our past, giving me a love of history. My interest piqued, I read Robert Henry's *The Story of the Confederacy* and then Robert Penn Warren's *Wilderness* and the Cass Mastern episode in that great American political novel, *All the King's Men*. And then reading such works as *I'll Take My Stand* by a group of agrarian writers and *Let Us Now Praise Famous Men* by James Agee, realizing that agrarian life in the South had diverged from the vision of American life that Jefferson imagined and was spoiled by the exploitation of Black labor as well as poor whites under another form of exploitation in tenant farming. And then for most of my life reading books on the Civil War as they came to me, not quite comprehending my sympathy for the South in the face of the stupendous bigotry and wrongness of slavery. Some of my teachers were apologists for the South, citing states' rights and sectionalism as the primary causes of the war.

Born in 1905, my father arrived soon enough after the war to know some of its survivors. After growing up on the family farm near the now-eclipsed farming community of Worthington in eastern Jefferson County, he moved in his early teens to Crescent Hill by way of Pewee Valley with his mother and three siblings after his father died in 1916. In the sleepy Louisville suburb of Pewee Valley he lived next door to the Confederate home, recently the subject of a book published by the University Press of Kentucky. When I asked him whether he could recall any stories, he said that he had been too young and could remember only some slack old-timers sitting in rockers on the porch. Fifty-one years after Appomattox, these would be among the last survivors on either side during our most destructive and defining war.

When I asked him and my uncle Orin about family connections to the Civil War, I was first told that none of our direct ancestors fought on either side. I had read a memoir of a Southern general named Richard Taylor, the son of a president. Though he had roots near Louisville, he was from another branch of the family and had spent most of his life in Louisiana. But I did hear a sketchy tale of one Taylor who had been shot out of a tree in an orchard behind the family house at Shop Spring near Worthington. When I asked why, Uncle Orin said for "singing Rebel songs," which I now understand as shorthand for stirring up secessionist sentiment in the neighborhood and, as I learned even more recently, violating his signed parole. The strand of memory had been broken. My father's own father had died relatively young, and my father himself was only ten or twelve when he lived next to the aging Confederates, just enough time to break the transmission of more vital family history.

The story my uncle told was that the victim's mother had seen a federal patrol coming up the lane to their farmhouse and that she had alerted her convalescent son, who bolted out the back door to hide. He had climbed a tree in the orchard and was shot out of it when he refused to come down. Uncle Orin told another story, this one even less detailed, involving a Taylor who had been captured and sent to a prison camp, where he was struck on the head by a pistol or rifle butt. He survived many years after the incident but was what his people delicately described as "touched" or "simple."

That was the substance of what I had learned from my elders and was not even sure what the combatants' names were or what their exact relationship to me was until I read Russell Chamberlain's mini-history of the Worthington community. As far as my father knew, no one in our family had fought on either side of the conflict. In fact, there had been participants on both.

Two of Reuben Taylor's grandsons, Reuben (called Ben) and Henry, enlisted in the Confederate army early in the war. Henry was badly wounded at the battle of Shiloh fought on April 6–7, 1862, taking one shot in the shoulder and another that broke his leg above the knee. Led on a horse away from the battle, he was hidden in a thicket until he could receive medical attention. When he was able to travel, he returned home by river steamer, having been required to sign a parole that he would not serve again in the Confederate army. After a slow recovery, he supposedly violated his parole by drilling some young boys in the area. One day, in the post office at Harrods Creek a few miles from Louisville, he witnessed a federal patrol of four cavalrymen leading a prisoner, remarking, as Chamberlain reports, "By Gawd, it would take at least ten damn Yankees to carry me to town." A man reportedly named Stonestreet informed on him, and next day the Provost Marshal in Louisville sent a detachment to the family farm. Warned that riders in blue were in the front yard, Henry, according to this account, strapped on his gun belt and ran from the house, hiding in a plum thicket. The federal detachment consisted of ten men commanded by a Captain Riddell. When Riddell and his sergeant approached the thicket, Henry, knowing that they were coming for him, attempted to fire his pistol, but the cap had fallen from its nipple and the pistol misfired. Before he could fire again, the sergeant shot him through the heart with his carbine, killing him instantly.

Apparently feeling some conscience about killing a wounded man in the presence of his mother, Riddell returned to the house and had his men place the dead man on a bed. When the horrified mother accused the captain of murdering her son, he replied that he had shot in self-defense. Then one of the detachment rushed up to report that a body of armed men was approaching the house. Captain Riddell ordered his men to line up in front of the farm entrance with their guns leveled at the oncoming riders. They turned out to be Union men returning from a nearby church. One of them was Henry's cousin, Manlius Taylor, wearing his federal uniform. The others were Billy Chamberlain, 16th Indiana, and two other local men named Dorsey, all of them on leave from the Union army. Manlius Taylor defused the situation by stating that they were returning from church and in fact were unarmed. Shortly after the Union detachment left for Louisville, a party of nearly two dozen neighbors arrived at the house, their leader hot-headedly intent on pursuing the detachment and shooting or hanging them all before they could reach the safety of Louisville. A cooler head, Jacob Chamberlain, acknowledged that the detachment could be caught but that given any provocation, Col. Dent, the area commander, would ride out in force and leave not a house or barn standing and who knows how many hanging. The party dispersed.

These accounts provided more grist for my speculations. First was the idea of the brothers' war, the often-invoked drama of divided loyalties within a single family, as in the case of Manlius and Henry, cousins. After this incident, however, Manlius renounced his ties to the Union, as history tells us many other loyal Kentuckians did for a variety of reasons, including the enlistment of African Americans into the military, an idea many loyal Kentuckians were not prepared to accept. In Manlius's case, it was, in his eyes, the unjust death of his cousin by those who presumably were his own comrades fighting to preserve the Union. His conversion may have also resulted from the zeal and mindlessness with which martial law was administered in the state as well as the bitterness harbored by both sides for real and sometimes imagined offenses. The right to speak one's mind freely was the birthright of every American. An atmosphere in which a nonjudicial authority could intervene to punish alleged slanders to Manlius and most other Kentuckians was unimaginable and abhorrent. Behind the provost marshal's decision to send ten and only ten men per Henry's boast bespeaks a perverse malice and spite that goes beyond our ordinary understanding of the usages of war. In Manlius's eyes, this offense was real. The fear of reprisals on a civilian population was also real and hardly isolated under the military authority that in fact governed Kentucky during the later stages of the war. This brand of suppression through a show of force must have soured the loyalty of many, as it apparently did Manlius. Though his family owned other human beings and he himself was probably proslavery, Manlius had enlisted as private in the 3rd Kentucky Cavalry (Union) in December of 1861. Ironically, he had served at Shiloh and could, in theory, have fired one of the shots that wounded his cousin.

Less obvious are the subtexts. One is that the tellers of the account that had been passed down orally through several generations remembered the names of the informer and those who commanded the arrest. Stonestreet is said to have bragged about what he'd done but suddenly packed up and moved to parts unknown by the time word got back to the Taylors. Whether Union or Southern in their loyalties, they were steeped in the Southern perspective that dominated the Kentucky mindset during the postwar era, and this, to some extent, colored their perceptions. It's also significant that the tale tellers knew and added what became of Captain Riddell. According to the account, Riddell was killed a few weeks later by one of his own company. Halting his men near a farm pond, Riddell had ordered his men to stay out of the water, though the day was hot, and men and horses were suffering from thirst. Returning from a nearby farmhouse, Riddell discovered one of his men had disobeyed his order and was standing waist-deep in the water. In a rage, Riddell drew his pistol and shot him. An instant later, a cousin of the dead soldier reciprocated by shooting Riddell himself. Blood, as the story and its sequel relate, is stronger than political allegiance. And memory is long.

The second account points up the tragic senselessness of this war, any war, this one coincidentally again involving water. Ben, or Reuben Taylor, grandson of the Revolutionary War Reuben, had been captured at the Battle of Chickamauga Creek (September 19–20, 1863). Sometime after Henry Taylor was killed, Henry's mother received a message from the federal authorities at the compound where her son was being held prisoner, directing her to send for him. According to the account, the unnamed camp (probably Camp Morton near Indianapolis) contained guards who were "cruel and brutal." Although there was abundant water available, prisoners were forbidden to drink except at given times of the day when, as the account states, they were driven like herds of cattle to slake their thirst. Again, the weather being hot and dry, prisoners suffered severely from forced deprivation of water. Ben Taylor asked one of the guards on an especially hot day for permission to go to the spring for water. When his request was denied, Taylor cursed the guard and started toward the spring. The guard quickly followed and struck Taylor on the head with the butt of his rifle, fracturing his skull and rendering him unconscious. He was given up for dead and left where he fell, but hours later, as he was being moved, he was found to be still breathing.

Ben Taylor was sent home after some weeks and lived for many years though his mind was deranged from the injury, and the wound never healed completely. Having the mental capacity of a small child, he was said to enjoy the company of children and in summer spent most of his time fishing along the banks of Harrods Creek. Lucy Spurgin, whom I knew as "Cousin Lucy" when I was in my teens and who was very close to my father, were nieces of Ben's parents and used to visit their aunt's farm. Lucy confessed that she was somewhat afraid of Ben, whose behavior seemed strange to her as a child. It was she who gave Russell Chamberlain details about Henry's death as well as accounts of another cousin, Walker Taylor, who gained notoriety as a Confederate spy. And Manlius's brother Hancock who joined the "mounted infantry" of John Hunt Morgan and participated in the raid north of the Ohio River into Indiana and Ohio (and who ironically studied law under Louisville attorney James Speed, brother of Lincoln's best friend and later the President's Attorney-General). Fewer people living in one place made for myriads of connections.

A few months after enlisting, brothers Manlius (Union) and Hancock (South) came home on leave. At a Sunday dinner for family and friends their father Dabney suddenly thrust a question on his son, "Manlius, why the devil are you fighting against your brother?" Manlius responded in an equally loud tone, "Well, by Gawd, he is fighting against me, isn't he, Pa?" The account states that the topic of conversation was changed by other guests and did not come up again. In its way, this story points up the larger absurdity of relations and countrymen divided for reasons, mostly political, some conscience-driven, that divided a nation, a state, a family. When Manlius died in 1908, he was buried in the Zachary Taylor National Cemetery on Brownsboro Road outside Louisville. On the marker is inscribed "Capt. Manlius Taylor, C.S.A." No mention is made of his previous and more conspicuous service with the Union in Company G, 3rd Kentucky Cavalry. He had fought brother against brother, cousin against cousin, at Shiloh where his kinsman Henry was wounded. Who knows how Henry's death affected his allegiance to the federal government in view of what happened to his cousin? In 1908 many Kentuckians whose families suffered during the war carried deep enmity against the federal government, southern Democrats dominating state politics for generations to come.

It was when I started researching material on the life of Confederate guerrilla Sue Mundy that a fuller, less fragmented image of the Civil War in Kentucky began to take form. I had seen a photograph of a young man in a Confederate uniform in a coffee table collection called *Views of Louisville*, published by *The Courier-Journal* in 1971 and edited by the late Sam Thomas, a friend since high school days at Atherton High School. The portrait, an enlarged daguerreotype, depicted a handsome young man sitting with legs crossed, armed and wearing a Confederate uniform topped by a hat that sported a plume. He was staring into the camera lens and appeared self-assured and, oddly, given later knowledge of his experience, innocent. That photo instantly sparked my interest and led to my seeking out every print source I could find—articles in history journals, references in Civil War histories and biographies, diaries, memoirs, and finally military records and accounts of courts-martial housed in both Kentucky and the National Archives in Washington, D.C. Over a period of nearly thirty years, on and off, I worked to shape the material into a novel, *Sue Mundy: A Novel of the Civil War*.

Here was a young man, Marcellus Jerome Clarke, product of a middle-class Kentucky home, who idealistically joined the Confederate army, was captured, escaped, and served meritoriously with John Hunt Morgan's cavalry until Morgan's death in September of 1864. Returning to Kentucky disillusioned and dislocated, he joined a band of guerrillas and eventually became their leader—at least the person by whom they were identified. He himself became the victim of notoriety and politics when the pro-Union editor of the *Louisville Daily Journal*, George D. Prentice, sought to depict him as a woman in order to embarrass the Union authorities in whom, along with many other loyal Kentuckians, he had lost confidence. Prentice's two sons had joined the Confederacy, and one was killed riding with Morgan. When Clarke, whom Prentice recast as the infamous Sue Mundy, was captured in a barn where he had hidden to nurse a wounded comrade, the Union authorities in Louisville lost little time in finding him guilty before a military tribunal, which denied him the right to summon witnesses and publicly hanged him two days after his capture, still shy of his twentieth birthday. To balance the record, I read accounts of courts-martial in which witnesses described the murders, rapes, and robberies that went on under the guise of fighting a war.

But it was research at the time of the Lincoln bicentennial for a commissioned ten-thousand-word article examining the President's Kentucky connections, and later, a collection of sonnets on Lincoln, that led to discovering some of the ironies and tragic consequences of the war. In Kentucky, Lincoln was, and to some extent still is, its least favorite son. Why? His political maneuverings to keep Kentucky in the Union were every bit as sensitive and artful as those depicted in Spielberg's *Lincoln* in which the president shepherded the Thirteenth Amendment into law. It is arguably Kentucky that shaped the character of a leader who emerged as our greatest president, for his impressionable earliest years were spent in Kentucky, and Kentuckians and former Kentuckians, including his wife Mary Todd of Lexington, influenced him as friends and mentors through the remainder of his life. These included his three law partners, his best friend Joshua Speed of Farmington, his political *beau ideal* Henry Clay, and many other former Kentuckians with whom he was associated in Illinois and Washington D.C. When he was a still a child, his father's scorn for slavery prompted a move to the free territories and states, giving Lincoln a distaste for slavery that seasoned into the complex forces leading to emancipation. An autodidact, Lincoln overcame the limitations of his childhood on the frontier, including a lack of formal schooling, a fully illiterate household, and extreme poverty until he was in his twenties and practicing law. On one of his rare visits to Kentucky in 1847, he witnessed the inhumanity of slavery at slave pens within blocks of his in-laws' home. In his debates with Stephen A. Douglas he grounded his position on slavery in morality since slavery predicated its treatment of Blacks on the supposition that they were not fully human but simply transferable property and that they existed only to serve their betters. Lincoln at the time adopted a more central position. He skillfully used his taste for oratory, and storytelling as a device of persuasion had its roots in the traditions of speech-making and advocacy so central to Kentuckians of his day.

Not all of Kentucky's folkways and political views were compatible with Lincoln's own sense of justice and morality. One of the ironies of his career is that he never within his lifetime won the full allegiance and support of Kentucky, his native state. So strong was the South's antipathy for the man that the harlequin cabbage bug, a common garden pest, was known as the "Abe Lincoln bug." Even today, that respect from many seems grudging. Despite his successes in the Northeast and Midwest, from the time he revived his political career on the eve of the Civil War until his untimely death, neither he nor the fledgling Republican Party was ever popular in Kentucky, in part owing to the commonwealth's deep emotional and familial bonds with the South but largely because of his stands on slavery. During the 1860 presidential election, for example, in his native state Lincoln polled the fewest votes of four candidates, receiving only three in his home county of Larue and only five in his wife's home county of Fayette. In the presidential election of 1864 he was outvoted in Kentucky by his Democratic opponent, Gen. George B. McClellan. His views on slavery threatened what many Kentuckians regarded as the state's economic well-being since it would deprive slaveholders of what they regarded as their property without compensation.

Lincoln supported the doctrine of neutrality early in the war to keep Kentucky within the Union, skillfully steering political sentiment in Kentucky to keep it from defecting, realizing that many Kentuckians straddled the issues, being both pro-Union as well as proslavery and pro-states' rights. His policies succeeded in preventing Kentucky from joining the Confederacy, at least until the Confederacy ceased to exist as a political entity. Later in the war, the president adopted a policy of emancipation and sanctioned the enlistment of Blacks in the Union army, an act that outraged many Kentuckians, including respected Union war heroes like Col. Frank Wolford, who was arrested for his alleged treasonous protest against validating African Americans as fully human and reliable as soldiers. These policies created a radical shift in loyalties among former Unionists in the state, and Lincoln, to quote one critic, became a "tyrant and a usurper," undermining basic constitutional concepts of property that underlay prevailing notions of white superiority. Added to other real and perceived abuses of constitutional law, many Kentuckians felt betrayed and shifted their allegiance to the Southern cause, largely on the issue of slavery. They felt that emancipation was a state matter, deeply resenting any interference by the federal government. The anti-federal fallout set a political tone that defined a political mindset in Kentucky, and, for better or worse, in large part defines it today.

But the price for the state and its future was high. Emancipation not only created a massive defection from the Republican Party but also cost decades of progress during the post-war boom that saw the country grow, for the most part, into an industrialized powerhouse with widespread educational opportunities and rewarding careers that had an increasingly urban orientation as well as a higher standard of living for most of its neighbors, North and South. Tied to its lifeblood in agriculture, the state that was economically strong and forward-looking before the war lagged in education and adapting to a manufacturing economy. Progress was impeded by one-party rule, reflecting the electorate's disdain for the Republican Party during the period of Radical Reconstruction. With few exceptions, the state also suffered from a lack of strong leadership that did comparatively little to produce an educated citizenry adapted to the demands of the twentieth century. The state that showed such promise before the war lost its stride. It had lost some of its most talented youth to the war and others in failing to promote public well-being after the war. In the eastern portion of the state where an economic bonanza came to the mountains, few of the natives prospered as timber and coal interests in effect made a colony of much of the region in which too little of the wealth trickled down to its producers.

A portrait of Kentucky before and after the Civil War represents a study in contrasts. Before the war it ranked eighth in population among the thirty-two states. Louisville, with a population of 43,000, was the tenth largest urban area in the country and the third largest city in the South. Its population ranked ninth in the nation and seventh place in the value of farms. The third largest slave-holding state, Kentucky was one of the most prosperous, based largely on its diversified agriculture—first in hemp production, second in tobacco and corn. The value of its livestock, including horses, mules, and hogs, ranked high, sixth in the nation. The state was an impressive place in 1860. In the area of education, Kentucky had one of the best public education systems in the South. It excelled in higher education, having early established law and medical schools at Transylvania University, the sixteenth oldest college in the country. Lexington was known as the "Athens of the West." On the eve of the Civil War, there were other strong colleges like Centre, Georgetown, and St. Joseph's. As state historian James Klotter has pointed out, Kentucky was renowned as the nursery of national leaders, including Henry Clay, Abraham Lincoln, Jefferson Davis, John C. Breckinridge, Richard M. Johnson, John J. Crittenden, and Zachary Taylor. At the same time it was one of the largest slave-holding states, one of every five Kentuckians being held in bondage.

Strongly rooted in the idea of Union, Kentucky's business, blood, and cultural ties gave it strong associations with the South, accounting for its ambivalent and unusual political stance of loyalty to the Union but strong endorsement of states' rights and slavery, property in human beings serving as one of the chief but unsustainable sources of its economic wealth. As President Lincoln so memorably said, in regard to Kentucky's strategic importance to the Union, "I think to lose Kentucky is nearly the same as to lose the whole game." Or, more famously, "I would like to have God on our side but must have Kentucky." Kentucky was more important to the nation in 1860 than it has been any time since and not simply because of its strategic geo-political position. The question to answer is *why*.

By the fall of 1864 Kentucky, though no longer a battlefield where armies clashed, was fighting its own uncivil war of neighbor against neighbor in a nineteenth-century preview of Iraq. A guerrilla war threatened every aspect of public life, one in which people were separated not by religion or ethnic origins but by political ideology and family loyalties. Church congregations split on the issue of slavery. Families split up, sometimes even changing the spelling of their names to indicate sides. The splits fueled the guerrilla war in which opponents as often as not knew the persons they were shooting at. In this war without two armies, the most notorious Confederate guerrilla was Marcellus Jerome Clarke, alias Sue Mundy, whose band terrorized much of the central region of the state. In order to quell this "little war" and keep Kentucky in the fold, President Lincoln tapped Stephen Burbridge, a young war hero who distinguished himself at Vicksburg and later surprised and scattered John Hunt Morgan's raiders at Cynthiana in June of 1864.

A Kentuckian, a graduate of Georgetown College and the Kentucky Military Institute (my father's alma mater), Burbridge was appointed by President Lincoln as commander of the Military District of Kentucky on August 7, 1864. Among his duties was to win the war against guerrilla bands that terrorized the state. His method was to meet violence with violence. On October 26, 1864, he issued an order to shoot any guerrillas encountered on sight, earning himself the name "Butcher" Burbridge. He arrested several newspaper editors critical of President Lincoln. He enacted a series of repressive measures that had little effect on guerrillas or outcome of the war but outraged the civilian populace, alienating many by his unreflecting brutality, including reprisal shootings, fifty or so, for the deaths of Union men at the hands of guerrillas. Under his infamous Order 59, four guerrillas were to be executed for every Union man killed. Many of those executed were *bona fide* Confederate prisoners of war, selected by lot from military prisons. He later ordered that any Confederate sympathizer within five miles of a guerrilla raid be subject to arrest and banishment.

Overzealous and insensitive to the effects his actions had on ordinary citizens, General Burbridge did much to alter public opinion in Kentucky for a whole generation of Kentuckians. In addition to suspending civil rights, he became implicated in what has been described as the "Great Hog Swindle" in which all surplus hogs in Kentucky were to be sold to the U.S. Government, prohibiting their export from the state. Though Lincoln finally removed Burbridge from command in February of 1865, the damage had been done, especially since the President appointed another radical Republican, Gen. John Palmer, to replace him. The collective result of these measures was a general antipathy for the federal government, the legacy of which arguably persists in Kentucky politics. In serving the nation so ably by keeping Kentucky in the Union, Lincoln lost the allegiance of many in his home state through Burbridge's repressive policies. Divided first by allegiances to one government or the other, Kentucky for a time suffered under a harsh military regime that severely limited the constitutional rights of free speech and conscience, of *habeas corpus*—liberties that most Americans take for granted. Such measures chaffed against patriotic and freedom-loving Kentuckians. Newspapers were suppressed for their editorial views. Citizens were imprisoned or deported from the state. Historian Lowell Harrison summarized the effects of martial law in Kentucky during the final year of the war:

> Intense hatred of the federal interference in state and national elections, extortion by Federal officers, suppression of the press, slave stealing, the use of black troops, the institution of martial law, and theft of all that was edible—treatment like that of a conquered province.

The presidential election of 1864 reflected this widespread disaffection for its native son, now regarded as perhaps our nation's greatest president for preserving the federal Union and manumitting four million persons from the onus of slavery. When free elections resumed, Kentuckians showed their disdain by voting consistently Democratic, siding with her sister states in the defeated South. Many perceived Emancipation as unlawfully depriving citizens of their property. It is a sad reminder of the perceived betrayal of trust that Kentucky did not ratify the Thirteenth

Amendment abolishing slavery until 1976. This perception of injustice by slave owners and their sympathizers so stained the legacy of Lincoln that Kentuckians voted overwhelmingly with the Solid South for decades, identifying themselves with their neighbors to the south. One-party rule was costly, for it stymied progress and encouraged complacency and a false sense of well-being. Kentuckians did not elect a Republican governor until 1896 when William O. Bradley, defeated by Confederate general Simon Bolivar Buckner in the previous election, electioneered his way into office.

Because I am not caught up in the urgencies of the Civil War or its aftermath, my own transformation has been more gradual, more ambivalent, less grounded in certainty. Causes are never quite so explainable or definitive as history tends to paint them. Human motivation to choose one loyalty over another is as complex and diverse as each of our individual lives, though the atmosphere in which those choices are made owes much to what's in the air, the mood, world view, and attitudes of the people around us as well as the experiences that shape our own lives. As I think of my Taylor antecedents and relations—Henry, Ben, Manlius, Hancock, and others—all in a sense my fathers, I recognize their insistence on self-determination as a guiding force even though they did not extend that right to those they owned. I admire their adherence to their values and their willingness to act on them—something our own era seems to discount in a world that is more determined by events we neither control nor even fully understand, a world of bystanders. Col. Wolford had the luxury and will to act on his convictions regardless of consequences though few, including me, would laud his views today. I also recognize that however right the Union cause as framed by Abraham Lincoln and the policies executed by his generals, abuses and injustices occurred such as those described in the rural community of Worthington. I know that the unnamed federal prison certifiably had its counterpart in Andersonville, Georgia, and Richmond, Virginia, that Burbridge to some degree had duties imposed on him from above, however draconian the way in which he chose to perform them. Like many Kentuckians, I lament the loss of the seemingly simpler world that bred people who knew who they were and worked hard to extract a living, sustaining a way of life through the soil. Looking for lessons, I turn to the question of how the past forms and affects our present.

I am waiting to read a new installment of Civil War history that will analyze the effects of Kentucky's nearly full turn to the South in the postwar years. What was gained and what was lost? To what extent did events during the Civil War in Kentucky shape its future? To what extent was the development of the state thwarted by its belated "secession"? To what degree has the disillusionment with one president and his policies fostered a national perception of Kentucky as rigidly conservative and often reactionary in its choice of political leadership? To what extent do inherited attitudes about race impede our progress? To what extent did the Commonwealth's slippage in education and economic development contribute to the hardships now encountered by many of its citizens? To what extent does the exodus of many of our brightest derive from a lack of vision and poor decision-making among our elected officials since the second half of the nineteenth century? These are the questions that need to be answered fully to understand the role of the Civil War in shaping Kentucky's destiny. Whatever the answers, it is clear that the past is still with us. It shapes our beliefs and attitudes, our politics. It also shapes our opportunities and vision for the years to come. It can bind or limit us or become the scaffolding on which to build a full and sustainable future.

After my father's death in 1974, I found two large, framed lithographs, one of Robert E. Lee, the other of Stonewall Jackson, that I keep even now—figures revered in the South by my father's generation—though I have long recognized that the way of life for which they fought was fundamentally flawed. They were published in the 1890s and depicted these gray warriors sympathetically, even nobly, as though candidates for sainthood. Why had he kept them? He was too much a believer in justice to accept the notion of racial inferiority. Since childhood he had Black friends in the Worthington neighborhood. I had never heard him express a racially insensitive sentiment and knew that several of his clients from Worthington were Black. With Emancipation one of his Taylor ancestors donated land on which the Taylortown Baptist Church was founded, many of its members previously owned by those same ancestors.

As a young lawyer back from Washington, where he'd worked in the Department of Justice, my father announced as a candidate in a primary election for magistrate of District One in 1937, his only foray into politics. My brother Douglas shared a letter of endorsement that appeared in the paper from a member of the Black community in Berrytown, a Republican. The writer stated that Joe H. Taylor had always "shown a kindly and sympathetic spirit toward people of our race," treated African

Americans with dignity and respect, that he was the community's friend, "always willing to lend a helping hand," and that the writer encouraged his Republican friends to vote for a Democrat—this at a time when Southern Democrats were associated with voter suppression and economic exploitation of Blacks. Another participant at the meeting where candidates were discussed affirmed that he had "known Mr. Taylor since he was a little boy at Worthington when we nicknamed him Buzz." He went on to say that he had always been a "straightforward, honest, and fair-dealing young man" and that for once in the speaker's life he planned to vote for a Democrat if he received the nomination. For whatever reason, he didn't receive the nomination. The only copy of his campaign poster I know of hangs in my daughter Julia's law office.

Buzz Taylor campaign poster.

Why had he kept the portraits? Perhaps out of loyalty to family members who had fought for the Confederacy. Maybe because of the romanticizing of the Lost Cause that occurred in Kentucky in the decades after the war, fueled by residual resentment toward Lincoln, who did not survive long enough to make good his policies of repatriating the South after a harsh military rule in Kentucky. Maybe because of that same streak of independence and distrust of government since the Whiskey Rebellion that had motivated many rural Kentuckians to resent the Union, then and now. Or maybe it was a childhood memory of beaten and harmless old warriors rocking feebly on the porch in Pewee Valley.

Raking the Coals

Picture me in my father's law office where I had been clerking two of my three years in law school, performing mostly menial tasks—toting or picking up papers in the circuit clerk's office, sitting in on depositions, driving one of my bosses home, occasionally researching case law in support of one legal position or another, matching factual situations to ongoing cases for solutions that would provide an arguable precedent for the case at hand. The actuarial tables in the appendix of the *Kentucky Revised Statutes* told me I would be doing essentially the same thing for the next 52.4 years—maybe with more responsibility and more money but essentially the same thing. On call for any odd jobs from any one of the six partners, the secretaries, or the office receptionist, I was the acting law librarian, my office being the meeting room with shelved walls of law reporters and a few legal treatises. I had passed the bar examination and was now an associate in the firm of Hogan, Taylor, Denzer, and Bennett. If I wanted it, I knew I had a job for life. *If I wanted it.*

I am sitting in my father's office as he finishes a phone call and directs his secretary, Juanita, to type up a pleading he has outlined. Standing maybe at five feet, she is a pert and efficient woman from the mountains with an inescapable twang. There is a momentary lapse in conversation as I wait for her to leave the room. He is in professional mode, all business and a little grave, the horn-rimmed glasses slipping down his nose, bespeaking sobriety and a serious-minded attention to matters at hand.

I am jittery—not so much nervous about what I've prepared to say as anxious about how he will take it. Never happy with my choosing English as a major, he had asked, "What are you going to do with *that?*" I recalled that when I was about to graduate from college four years earlier, the University of Kentucky had posted job offerings for each major. As you might expect, there were columns of opportunities for business majors and engineers, even students of psychology, not to mention elementary school teachers. Under "English majors" I found only one job opportunity: conducting interviews of suspected venereal disease patients for the U.S.

Department of Health. Uncertain about what to do and drawn to the academic life, I had gone on to earn a master's degree in English, thinking I was at least up to that and needing time to make a more definitive move. I completed the yearlong course of study and wrote a thesis on Truman Capote's *Other Voices, Other Rooms*, his brilliantly flawed first novel that went along with my flawed thesis paper. My last course obligation, a final exam in Literary Criticism, was postponed when news came that President Kennedy had been shot.

When I received my M.A. and was still living at home, my father finally asked what my plans were. I tried hard to find tactful ways to say I had none. I was too uncertain of myself to commit to earning a doctorate in English, and I sensed my sponsor had extended his largesse about as far as he was going to, especially in an area of study for which he saw no pragmatic outcome. I myself was not wholly wedded to the idea. I thought then that literary scholarship minced texts into something as granular and arid as oxen skulls in the high Sierras, applying language that was cloudy, jargon-filled, and remote. This was before I made my first attempt at teaching, a profession I came to love.

Kentucky Military Institute, 1924.

My father's own education beyond high school was a little sketchy, to this day another of the mysteries I encountered each time I probed beneath the surface, wishing the questions I had asked had fuller answers.

Here is what I gleaned. He had graduated from Kentucky Military Institute (K.M.I.) and gone on to University of Kentucky, where I understand he planned to study agriculture, an idea that comported with his interest in landscape architecture and horticulture. Caught up in the swirl of the Jazz Age, he had joined a fraternity, Phi Delta Theta. I know this because when I attended U.K. over thirty years later he told me I was a legacy for admission. However, for some reason—maybe its agriculture program was better or more adapted to his interests—he transferred to the University of Illinois, from which I'm assuming he graduated, because he was later admitted to law school at the Jefferson Law School—a predecessor to the modern University of Louisville School of Law—from which he received his degree in 1932. He must have had some reservations about his readiness to take on the responsibilities of a license because, as my mother related, he entered Cornell University in the fall of that year and studied for two more semesters. I was skeptical about this until Willis uncovered his transcript indicating that during a year of enrolling in ten courses he had earned a few Bs and a spate of gentlemanly Cs. He said little when I asked him about attending. When I quizzed my mother about it, she told me that though he had graduated as valedictorian of his class at K.M.I., completed a college degree, and earned an LL.B. from the Jefferson School of Law, he felt he needed a firmer grasp of the law. Maybe he saw these additional courses as preparation for the bar exam, icing on the cake. This is what prompted him to attend Cornell. One of the Louisville Bar directories I later found verified his attendance in Ithica. He himself was strangely silent on the subject. For whatever reason, he didn't finish a second degree—maybe because he ran out of money, maybe because he planned to marry my mother, maybe because he landed a job in Washington during the height of the Depression—or maybe a combination of all three.

My own case was different. Out of the blue one day my father, recognizing my uncertainty, suggested I could always go to law school, a proposition I hadn't permitted myself to consider. The Vietnam War was gaining momentum in 1964, and the prospect of being drafted or going to Officer Candidate School (O.C.S.) loomed large on my narrowing horizon. My brother Douglas, two years my junior, had attended O.C.S. on graduating from college and had been sent to Vietnam as an ordnance officer, a lieutenant. So I entered law school by default, rationalizing that a law degree would open an array of career possibilities or that maybe I would take to it. The study of law might offer triumphs and challenges; the practice of law was a cipher.

My deeper self harbored the desire to write. Since high school I imagined myself becoming a writer, not a poet so much as a novelist, studying life from the sidelines and recording what I saw. I had a romantic view of the writer as a sentient sponge that sopped up life around him and released it in memorable language. I did not think of it as hard work, though I was later reminded of a statement writer friend Ed McClanahan uttered at a hotel bar one night: "I love being a writer—it's the paperwork that gets me down." Because I had a master's degree, I was not required to take the Law School Admissions Test, a test whose logic section I could not have passed, then or now. But my background in language and writing was enough to carry me through law school. During those three years I ran scared, making my best grades in the courses I hated most—taxation and the Uniform Commercial Code, for example—courses pretty far removed from vibrant humanity. It came as no surprise that my favorite course was Jurisprudence, a body of readings in the philosophy of law that not so coincidentally tended toward literature. In college I never seriously saw myself in law school, never had taken a course in political science or consulted a prelaw advisor about a legal career. My curriculum was *Beowulf* and as much Hemingway and company as I could get because I thought that reading the moderns would show me how to join them. Overnight, it seemed, my studies changed direction from literature to law, from Sylvia Plath to torts, from the Beat poets to contracts and the law of real property and the abstract concept of livery of seisin, the medieval transfer of land to another through passing something symbolic of real property, land, to a new owner, a twig or a handful of turf. The twig was in my hand. I gave up Signet and Penguin paperbacks for a legal pad. Like every other law student, I underwent indoctrination into a brave new world, one in which happenings were equated with legal consequences for which the measure became whether individuals were either criminally or civilly answerable. Legal study was at first a comforting reality since it seemed to rest on a foundation of certainty, but it was also a limiting view of the world, excluding, among other things, aesthetics, the whimsical, the random, the spiritual. It regarded the world purely in material terms, and its language I found precise but stunted, antiseptic, and limiting, undernourished. No metaphor here. No equivocal expression. No extension of understanding through words exploited for their richness. I recently ran across a statement by novelist Scott Turow, who said of his own experience that reading case law was like stirring concrete with one's eyelashes.

But fear is a great motivator, and I feared not so much flunking out as facing my father as a failure. I did not want to let him down. So I studied harder than I'd ever studied, before or after. For the first time since starting college I studied on Friday nights. I had a routine of going to the law library, where I crossed my legs on a library table and briefed cases or caught up on reading for my classes. What I could not accomplish with gifts of understanding I sought to survive with total immersion. And Grace Von Allman, the librarian, graciously overlooked my violation of library rules about keeping my feet on the floor. It seems my head was also free to perch where it would. After the library closed at 10:00 PM, I would reward myself at a local bar, usually a nearby college hangout called The Zanzibar for a few extracurricular beers.

After the initial shock of learning a new way to learn, I suffered from deprivation of rich and unpasteurized language. I can remember that my greatest pleasure after completing finals each semester was reading a carefully selected novel, something as far as I could stray from the stuffiness I was breathing daily. I can remember after the last final one December devouring William Styron's *The Confessions of Nat Turner*, savoring each word that lacked an identifiable legal consequence. I imagined myself plotting with Nat, entering the complex and confused world that motivated an enslaved person to take up arms against those who enslaved him.

So three months after law school and successfully passing the bar, I was faced with the hardest decision I had ever made—informing my father that I wanted to leave the law, that "cruel and jealous mistress," and go off to teach. "What are you going to do with English?" he had asked. Now I had an answer though not, to him, a very satisfactory one. I remembered the snarky dictum that those who cannot do teach, an attitude I suspected he subscribed to. He must have thought my little mutiny an affront to common sense. I couldn't tell him that I dreamed of becoming a writer. I couldn't tell him, as I would later know after years of prelaw advising, that English is an ideal major for law school. The truth was I loved language and books, not the sterile and precise language of the law but words applied to expand reality rather than shrink it down to prescribed legal outcomes. The world I wanted to study was neither so predictable nor fixed. I came to think of legal thinking as a little tyranny, a little Bastille that needed storming to release its prisoners. Immersed for three years in a legal view of the world, involuntarily I was held hostage to a single way of regarding the world, a milder form of bondage. I can remember a little homily of Lincoln's on the credenza in the hallway of the law office—"A lawyer's time is his stock in trade," and I had deluded myself that I could practice law during the day and devote myself to writing at nights. I quickly discovered the futility of that pipe dream.

One of my classmates had taken a teaching job at a junior college and provided me with the name of a placement service in Memphis. It wasn't long before I received notice of a job opening at a little junior college in Mississippi, a state I knew only as the home of William Faulkner with a reputation for substandard education even lower than Kentucky's. For me it was a means of escape, and a whole new prospect of the future had suddenly dawned. All I had to do was gracefully sever the ties that bound me to a profession for which I was not suited, especially since I was not in the least competitive or adversarial. All I had to do was confront my father.

So here I was, having recently celebrated passing the Kentucky bar exam and now meeting with my father to chuck it all in. When I came into his office, he was bent over a stack of papers, his horn-rimmed glasses halfway down his nose, his coat neatly folded over a padded chair, tops of magnolias by the courthouse visible from his window three stories below—a path by now all too familiar to me.

"Dad," I began, "I have something I need to tell you." His eyes rose from the abstractions on the page to gaze at his son, who must have appeared serious for once. For a moment he looked as though he had divined what was coming. Then he gave me his full attention.

"I have an offer of a teaching job that begins after Christmas," I said, fibbing a bit to soften the blow since I'd already accepted the job. "It's at a little junior college in the Mississippi Delta, and I've promised them I'd be there before the semester begins."

I could see him absorbing the news, reimagining his elder son not in a courtroom but behind a lectern or desk, a pile of paperbacks in a dingy office off the quad, on his own, paying his own way, and doing what he thought he wanted to do at a time when college students were fighting to escape the draft.

At that time teaching jobs with a master's degree—not to mention a law degree—were plentiful. A junior college in the remoteness of the Mississippi Delta was the closest thing, I later sensed, to a foreign country within the continental United States, a vast alluvium that was monotonously flat with small towns and, I later discovered, few if any places to buy a beer, much less sociably drink one. I'd requested my transcript and recommendation from the law school dean, who generously perjured himself with my qualifications. All I needed to do was placate my parents, load my bags and a few books into my VW hatchback, and head several hundred miles to the southwest.

There was a long silence between us as his wheels turned, and I cushioned myself for outrage. To my surprise and relief, his face didn't redden. There was no barking. He received what I had just told him as though he was an appellate judge taking a brief under advisement, though his picture of my world had dramatically altered in only a few words. After absorbing the news and running the variables through his legal mind, he visibly relaxed, responding in a rational way with questions. When did I plan to leave? Was I sure this is what I wanted to do? And many more as the idea sank in, giving both of us time to adjust to a new climate, a new reality.

These and similar questions I pondered for months myself until I had adapted to life as a recovering lawyer, the best career decision I ever made. Why did I leave the law? Beyond my hearing, my mother and father must have discussed my throwing over what I'd worked fairly hard to acquire—a legal education and a secure future performing useful and honest work. My mother was convinced I left the law because I had to wear a tie each day and put in an appearance at the office on Saturday mornings—a tradition that cut into weekend recreations. My father, I believe, never quite saw me as the successor to the law practice he'd built over decades, nor was he self-centered enough to consider that I would profit from his reputation for no-nonsense honesty in a profession downrated for its confusion of eloquence and conniving with justice and fair dealing. I was not adversarial. I had no desire to become the professional, as one smooth-tongued classmate over a beer or two had once described himself: "My name is Terrence Noe, and I'm a hog lawyer from Mt. Vernon, Indiana. I have silver on my tongue and manure on my feet, but sometimes I get them reversed."

Though he never said it, I believe I had my father's tacit understanding and consent, not from a careful weighing of alternatives but from personal experience. Law, after all, had not been his first choice for a livelihood, and he must have harbored similar feelings over his forty-year career as I've discovered many other lawyers do. Yet he had found a way to balance his love of horticulture with the sensible stability of practicing law. At some level he saw that my dilemma was less accommodating, that I couldn't flirt with literature or creative writing and draft legal pleadings or quote Shakespeare standing before a jury. He was my judge and jury, and to his credit, he accepted with generosity and restraint a verdict from which there was no appeal. At bottom I believe he wanted for me what would give the most long-term fulfillment, and though he couldn't fully imagine that other world, he accepted the landscape that he saw only hazily before me. We had reached an understanding—to put it in the language of legal settlements. Finally, we both knew we must all proceed according to our own lights or accept someone else's darkness.

Mistletoe

The parasitic plant that is often found in clusters of waxen green leaves and pearly berries among the crowns of roadside oaks and other deciduous trees in the Bluegrass and elsewhere in Kentucky was venerated by the ancient Druids as a cure for many ailments of old age and may, in some sinister way, have been related to human sacrifices. Its name derives from Anglo-Saxon "mistel," a word meaning "dung," and "tan," meaning "twig," commemorating a popular belief that this oddly placed plant sprang from the dung of birds that ate the berries and then perched in the host tree. Because it is evergreen during the vegetal desolation of winter, it became associated with eternal life and took on spiritual powers among the Scandinavians. Later, mistletoe was grandfathered into Christianity along with pagan customs, including decorated trees, door wreaths, and Yule logs. In Hertfordshire, England, it was removed from farmhouse kitchens on January 1 and burned, the belief being that without this ceremony there would be no crops. American Indians chewed it for toothaches, and tradition held that when hung around the neck, never ingested, it would cure such ailments as apoplexy, senile dementia, and palsy.

In the mythology of my childhood it was commonly believed that during Christmas, mistletoe, when hung in some prominent place inside the home—in ours from a small hook in the lintel above the French doors separating the living and dining rooms—was an invitation to a kiss. The custom dates back to early-seventeenth-century England when proper procedure required that a man pluck a berry as he kissed a girl who stood under it. When the last berry was gone, the kissing ended. As kids we steered clear of the festooned clump secured by a red ribbon since it drew mushy kisses from visiting aunts and older friends of my parents, especially when they had consumed a glass or two of my father's eggnog. At parties when we were a little older, it provided justification for stealing kisses from unsuspecting girls who ventured into its amatory zone. Among my earliest Christmas memories is my father's yearly ritual of trekking off to what we called "the country" and returning with jumbo chunks of mistletoe for our home and those of a few neighbors and friends.

The day before Christmas in 1974 I interviewed George Mercke, "Father" Mercke (pronounced "murky") as my father kiddingly called him. Spoken only half-facetiously, he would greet him with "Father Mercke! And what have you done for the good of the country today?" For which Mr. Mercke's invariable response was "Aww, Buzz," a chiding in feigned exasperation. George "Father" Mercke was our next-door neighbor on Pleasantview. My father, known to many of his friends as "Buzz," had recognized the need to make some record of their generation before it slipped completely away. Mr. Mercke, our neighbor of over thirty years, was a colorful character, irreverent and full of stories. He punctuated his recollections of hunting and camping out—of signing a doctor's register for Prohibition whiskey during his college days—with expletives and guttural self-amused laughs as he cast his memory back over his seventy-two years. He plopped it like a fly from his fishing rod into a pool of still waters and reeled back the past. Though he often presented an edge of gruffness, he was always tolerant and unfailingly kind to me, not because I never stepped into his flowerbeds or raised hell with his son Robert but because I had a certain immunity as the son of his close friend, a man he'd known long before I went to kindergarten.

My father had the knack of making things grow. When the hours of daylight lengthened with spring, he would remove the jeep's canvas top, change into old clothes, and work an hour or two before dark in the habitat he loved, the "country." The results were bounty enough to supply a small vegetable market or a detachment of French fusiliers. Never to my knowledge did he sell anything; his was the pleasure of bestowing. Often, he would simply place the vegetables or flowers on a porch or doorstep and move on—hence the nickname Buzz. Nor did he believe in conspicuous bestowal; he preferred anonymity and would dismiss thank-yous with self-deprecating good humor. He produced much more than any of us could consume, so he brought baskets of bounty to my Uncle Lawrence in St. Matthews and to Uncle Lawrence's neighbors, as well as his own neighbors and friends on Pleasantview, including George Mercke, whose stories I taped and rediscovered recently in a drawer swollen shut by July's humidity.

Mr. Mercke sat that day in a wing-backed chair in his living room before a fire fueled with maple and oak "scraps" he had delivered from "the factory," the woodworking business he and his brothers had inherited from their German-American grandfather. Greenery was strung along his mantelpiece, and a decorated tree stood at the other end of the room. In his gravelly drawl, he reminisced, recounting the expedition for mistletoe, one of my father's annual rituals that the two of them shared that year—and only that year.

Starting after breakfast on a cold December morning, they had driven east about twelve or fifteen miles to a farm in Worthington belonging to one of the farming families my father had known from the time when the area had been the largest producer of potatoes in the country: Simcoes, Littrells, Stutzenbergers, Ewings, and Sims (nicknamed "Buck," "Hymus," and "Beetle"). He himself had lived in the area until he was twelve and kept a lifelong relationship with the place, revisiting his childhood as well as friends and clients in the area.

"It was colder than hell," Mr. Mercke said, "sleeting and snowing."

Scouting around, they had found a likely tree in some upland pasture, probably one of the native oaks whose shade provided relief for cattle during the sweltering months of late summer. Most people we knew who fetched their own mistletoe turned up their noses at buying the expensive and paltry fist-sized clumps that sold in grocery lots and flower shops. But they went after it the easy way, shooting it out of the upper limbs with twenty-twos. My father, a purist, disdained the practice and thought of it as cheating. The clumps invariably were damaged in the fall and were always smaller. Mistletoe intact was infinitely more desirable than mistletoe riddled with shot, and he would not settle for anything less than jumbo clusters of the choicest specimens.

After parking the jeep, he unloaded his handsaw and a length of trotline, his only equipment. He may have suspected that something was amiss when they had trouble keeping their footing across the frozen ground with its slick of freezing sleet. Despite a cutting wind and bitter cold, he removed his work gloves for better gripping and prepared to scale the tree, pincering his legs around the trunk and hitching up to the closest limb, the rubber soles of his lightweight moccasins giving him flexibility but little support and less warmth.

"I stayed on the ground," Mr. Mercke said, "but your daddy was a tree climber. He'd go up a tree like a damn squirrel, and he'd take the mistletoe."

Picture the two of them, grandfathers both: Mr. Mercke, a hulking, slightly stooped man wearing a wide-brimmed hat and parka, his shoulders rounded with age, and my father, wiry and compact, in an old pair of khakis and a scruffy olive Army jacket. His crumpled felt hat still in place, he was gamely shinnying a tree in someone's vacant pasture during the dead of winter, a time when people of good judgment were sitting inside close to the heat, anticipating Saturday football or a travelogue to Hawaii. Or visiting with family. Instead, here he was in his sixties, painfully working his way up a sizable tree toward several clusters of mistletoe in its upper limbs. Taking advantage of every notch and crook in the branch work, he extended himself heedlessly onto brittle smaller limbs to get at the clumps, with their berries pale as tiny moons, their knobby stems and shiny, pale-green leaves that resemble clusters of elongated clubs on playing cards.

"And he'd take a piece of trotline," Mr. Mercke went on, "And drop it down. And then he'd pull the rope up, you know, like window sash. And then lower this big—hell, he cut limbs off—you know how big a chunks he'd gotten. Three or four of them would fill up the back end of that jeep. And I'd take the mistletoe and put it over in the jeep."

And then Mr. Mercke came to describe their particular predicament that day. "He got up there," he said. "Oh, it was awful. You know, the trees were icy, and he started getting tired, and his hands got so cold he couldn't come down."

As Mr. Mercke spoke and I watched the tiny wheels of the cassette spooling, I could imagine my father high up in the stripped tree, carefully lowering the last bunch of mistletoe down to his partner before it finally dawned on him to consider how he himself was to get back down. The brittle limbs were slick with a sheen of ice. He was cold, his hands and feet numb and aching. The risk he'd taken, almost without thinking, began to press on him with images of broken bones or worse. There was no reachable rescue, no cherry picker on a fire truck to which he might step with impunity. So he clung to the limbs and tried to puzzle a way free of what seemed at the very least certain injury. I can imagine Mr. Mercke, exhausted himself, at the base of the tree, stiffening with cold and wondering how he was going to get his friend to the hospital.

"Why hell, I can't come get you," he shouted up to the behatted figure stuck in the skein of limbs. "What are you going to do?" And then as an aside to me, almost an apology, as he placed himself at the foot of the frozen tree again, "The rope wouldn't hold him, you know it isn't strong enough." The only remedy he could think of was for my father to restore circulation in his bare hands.

"Buzz," he yelled up to the figure hugging a thigh-sized limb maybe thirty feet off the ground. "Open up your jacket and get your hands inside next to your stomach. Maybe they'll get warm enough. I'll stand down below you, and if you fall I'll break the fall. But we'll both probably be dead then."

After a long period of silence, my father, as best he could, pushed one hand into his jacket while Mr. Mercke crooked his neck upward, waiting. And then the other hand. The snow was still falling, so thick he could barely see the jeep maybe thirty yards away. And then the dark shape gripping the limbs started to inch down, looking back over his shoulder or down between his legs, taking advantage of forks where he could find them, and then finally getting close enough to dangle some moments from a horizontal limb before letting go. Mr. Mercke pulled him up from the hard ground and asked if he was all right. Although badly shaken, he said he was, and the two of them wasted no time in getting to the jeep.

"I'll bet it took him an hour to get out of that damn tree," Mr. Mercke was saying from his cushion by the fire. "And I was nearly freezing on the ground."

I can see the two of them—stiff and numb, a little unsteady—arranging the mistletoe in the back of the jeep, my father fumbling with the key to fit into the ignition, the engine turning over and catching, the two of them bouncing across the pasture and then along the rutted farm lane to the Brownsboro Road, where they take a left toward home, passing a few cars with their trunk lids tied down over protruding Christmas trees. The anemic heater under the dashboard on the shotgun side whirred impressively but generated very little heat inside the framed canvas in whose cold interior they could see their breath, little heads of white cauliflower, and raw daylight through slits around the plexiglass doors.

Sitting in the easy chair across from Mr. Mercke in that overheated room, I can retrace their course nearly forty years later as the Brownsboro Road turns onto U.S. 42 and widens to four lanes. They pass the Zachary Taylor Cemetery and Blankenbaker Lane, then make the long descent at Hubbard's Lane and back up past thick woods on both sides until they reach Indian Hills, the furthermost subdivision from Louisville that marks the unofficial dividing line between the last probing suburb and farmland. Then, just beyond Chenoweth Lane, no more than two miles from home, Mr. Mercke spots, off to the left, the Bauer's-since-1870 sign, the restaurant and bar that has been an East End landmark for nearly a century, a stopping place for travelers and local farmers—among them my father's father—as they hauled their produce to markets downtown half a century earlier. It is a modest frame building, its white siding broken by a matrix of elegant small-paned windows. A gas station and garage stand on one side, the east, a screen of Scotch pines and the barren white slopes of the Crescent Hill golf course on the other.

They are about to pass when Mr. Mercke says, "Good God, Buzz, we'll stop at Bauer's. We need a drink." So my father wheels into the lot, and the two of them, still shivering and looking vaguely disreputable, limp out of the weather, traipse through the dining area with its white-clothed tables (and who knows how many seated diners enjoying brunch) into the polished bar off the main dining room where they eye themselves in the long mirror broken by tiers of bottles with hooked spouts.

As Mr. Mercke remembers it, "So we went and got a doubleheader, of Old Grand Dad … good whiskey, you know, bonded. And we tossed it off, no chaser or anything." As he savors that memory, we can both feel that distilled fire as it hit the back of their throats and sluiced down, suffusing them with a brief but illusory neural warmth that must have left them gasping.

"And you could feel that heat," he said with satisfaction, "going right down to your stomach. And that's all we took, a double shot apiece."

Then the two of them, still exhausted, still cold, climb back into the jeep for the ride home, the hot bath, Mr. Mercke probably napping, my father at least relaxing after lunch, the mistletoe soon hanging above their respective lintels with maybe a few sprigs on the mantel, joking that night about their skirmish with disaster, confidence regained, eyeing the brittle knots of green mistletoe wrestled from the gray grip of winter a few days before Christmas, family home or on the way, the chill of that morning no longer physical but only the stuff of recollections by the fire.

And Mr. Mercke, laughing from somewhere deep in the winter of his chest, capping the story he'd told dozens of times and would tell again and again until only the tape was left to tell it.

"Damn, we got home, we were talking our heads off." Then reflecting, relishing again that moment when the double shot of whiskey at least partially rekindled that heat in their aging bodies. "That sure was the best drink, though. We needed that drink. That one time it was medicinal."

To this day, though both now are beyond the reach of snow and whiskey, each time my eye strays from the road to fix on the green bundle in the upper regions of an oak, each time I'm caught outside in biting cold underdressed, each time I can't back out of some predicament in which I have placed myself, I am in the tree shivering with my father or at its foot with Mr. Mercke searching for a way to persevere.

GRATITUDE

Fatherhood comes in many guises. Sometimes fathers are not fathers in the sense of blood descent. They can come through indirect kinship—in this case from a brother of the bride. Such was my mother's bachelor brother, Louis Dey, who lived with us in the house in Crescent Hill they both grew up in.

When my father married and made his way back to Louisville from Washington by way of Cleveland, where he worked for the Civil Aeronautics Board and then the Federal Land Bank, he entered the practice of law with Ed Hogan, a widowed lawyer some years his senior who represented several insurers defending claims arising from auto accidents. We took up residence on Pleasantview Avenue in my mother's childhood home with Uncle Louis—"Brother" as my mother called him—when I was about five, just getting ready for kindergarten at Emmet Field Elementary School five or six blocks away. If school offered some formal training, Louie Dey supplemented it with extracurricular tutoring—a love of art, a love of the possibilities of language, a world in which images and careful talk predominated.

Louis F. Dey, author's uncle.

Uncle Louis, as I called him, was a remarkable human being though, like all of us, not without flaws. His father, a clerk in Louisville's City Hall, died unexpectedly of a heart attack when Louis was twelve. In his late teens after graduating from high school, Uncle Louis found work at *The Courier Journal* and *Louisville Times*, Louisville's proud daily in two editions. There he spent his entire career, except for some time when he was drafted into the Army Reserve during World War II. After this brief hiatus, he was a newspaperman until his death in 1974, working in some menial start-up job initially and rising eventually to become the paper's art director.

Among other things, he was responsible for designing the masthead that the paper used for decades, and about which he was invited to lecture at Columbia University, known for having one of the finest journalism programs in the country. He also lectured on newspaper design at the University of North Carolina, the American Press Institute, and numerous seminars. Quite an accomplishment for someone who hadn't been to college. His mantra was making the paper visually appealing.

After his death, a letter to the editor from an unnamed colleague who knew him well described him as "a conscientious student of graphic art: … he created and directed the typographic style and excellence of appearance of both *The Courier-Journal* and *The Times*," his "taste being for simplicity and readability in the printed media." Another noted that he specialized in eye appeal, both in pictures and type choices. Barry Bingham, owner of the papers, sent him to Great Britain to study typography, format, column count, and aesthetics of the esteemed *Manchester Guardian*. As a consequence of his trip, the column count per page was reduced to five. The paper stock was grayed down slightly for the readers' ease. For a time the papers were ranked among the top ten in the nation.

There is a wonderful caricature of Louie Dey done by artist and cartoonist Paul Plaschke, a well-known regional painter working with him in the art department. The image, done in pencil and watercolor, profiles a seated figure wearing a vest with sleeves rolled up, the face with an intense expression, eyebrows arched critically, a pipe jutting out beneath a Roman nose, a natty striped tie, a hint of handkerchief protruding from the vest pocket. The only period he was absent from the paper was during World War II when he found himself a 38-year-old recruit at an infantry-training center at Camp Wheeler, Georgia. Fortunately, he was never shipped out and never saw combat.

I remember he had an affinity for water, walking a half-dozen blocks during workdays to take a dip at the downtown YMCA. He also cheered on my sister when she swam laps at the Crescent Hill Swimming Pool for her certification as a lifeguard. Occasionally, on summer Sundays my brother, sister, and I would pile into his 1951 Buick convertible and breeze ourselves while he drove us to Tucker's Lake in nearby Middletown. Riding to the lake under an invitingly open sky, I recall the four of us heartily singing some silly song or other. The lake, situated in what had been a quarry, was a refuge of suntan lotion and hot dogs, equipped with diving platforms whose topmost level I never summoned the courage to jump from. As if to justify her assessment of him as an "an odd duck," my sister Treva also confessed that once, when she was nine, he put her behind the wheel of his convertible and let her drive. As she steered, he cautioned her not to hit the stone pillars ahead of them. "Watch the pillars!" he shouted, only then realizing that she was too short to see them over the hood. From time to time he also invited me to accompany him to the Toddle House, a short-order hamburger joint in St. Matthews where the cook behind the counter grilled burgers and cooked hash browns in a metal ring—delicious.

In some ways "Louie," as adults in the family knew him, was as much a father as my blood father. Like him, he loved to grow things, in his case flowers, especially hostas and fancy-leafed caladiums—my favorite summer flower. He successfully learned to dig them up each winter, storing and restarting them each spring, a tricky undertaking that I have tried and failed. Lacking his skill, I now buy some at the nursery each spring and reinter them in my barrel-sized planters in the shade riddling my back steps.

Like my father, he lost his father at an early age. Unlike him, his mother was left with little means of support. At seventeen or eighteen when he graduated from Louisville Male High School, he went directly to work to support his mother and two sisters, sacrificing his own education. To compensate, he developed a lifelong love of reading, especially the history of civilizations and the evolution of the visual arts. He read *The New Yorker* each week with an almost vengeful determination and subscribed to the overseas edition of *The Manchester Guardian*.

A night owl, he seldom turned in before midnight. Always he had an artistic flair, a thirst to know the masters, collecting art books with dramatic views of the Sistine Chapel and classical Greece as well as the meaty sculptures hammered out or bronzed by Rodin. He sketched and sketched well. His brother-in-law—his sister Gene's husband, Terrell Dickey—was a successful commercial artist of print advertisements, as was his son, who was also a fine painter. I can't think of this other uncle without seeing four iconic roses in a tumbler on a white table in his backyard that I happened on one fall afternoon, Four Roses bourbon being one of his accounts. The photo soon appeared in an ad in *The New Yorker* or *Atlantic Monthly*. Uncle Terrell also hosted informal drawing classes in his basement studio, located in his comfortable home that doubled as his office, reception space, and design studio. Usually, a model was impressed into figure drawing, though sometimes landscapes were painted. The landscapes, I suspect, derived from photos, though his house bordered Cherokee Park, the atelier for any number of local *plein air* artists. Uncle Louis attended these sessions, becoming if he wasn't already, a proficient sketch artist.

Thanks to him, I have a sketch of myself done when I was one year old, something he probably dashed off in minutes, as I witnessed him do repeatedly when I was older. I also salvaged a study of a cathedral dome in oil done on his trip to Paris when I was in my teens. My sister owns a small portrait of my mother, his finest work, half in profile with a red rose in her hair. Another favorite painting is a larger landscape executed on art board with a cottage dominated by trees overborne by pasty clouds in a blue sky. Encrusted in grime, it was discovered when my mother cleared the attic of their home after his death in 1974. When as children we were punished for misbehavior, he would require the offender to hold a pose while he dashed off a sketch. Somewhere my mother stashed a trove of his sketches, and I hope they will eventually resurface. For more grave offenses, he would have us dig up weeds or rocks from his backyard flower beds. When he wanted to reward us, he let my brother and me choose a key from a box of discarded keys he kept on top of the refrigerator. We were indiscriminately young but soon were disenchanted with orphaned keys for which there were no locks. Later, he bestowed an allowance of 50 cents each week, enough for admission to the movies and some popcorn or juicy fruit candy. He also kept notebooks and files of now-lost sketches and darkroom photos that constituted a visual record of our childhoods in a chronicle of snapshots.

In addition to his love of art, Uncle Louis had a thirst for broader culture, a fuller, more rarified understanding of the world. Over the living room couch hung a large Piranesi print of Roman ruins, later supplanted by a more fashionable Andrew Wyeth print of Christina gazing out of a hayloft. During the time that my sister took ballet lessons, he would conduct her to performances of the Louisville Ballet at the Brown Theatre and dinner at the English Grill in the Brown Hotel. He also took her to see the Ballet Russe de Monte Carlo and road shows of the musicals whose originals he'd seen in New York. Once a year, along with Aunt Gene and Terrell senior he would catch the theatre train from Louisville to New York where he would indulge himself with a week of museum-going and Broadway plays. He must have especially loved musicals, for I grew up hearing LP recordings of *Annie, Get Your Gun, South Pacific, Oklahoma*, and *My Fair Lady*. He was also something of a clothes horse, returning from sophisticated New York to Louisville wearing shirts, ties, and suits from Brooks Brothers, Chipp, and J. Press, all top clothiers. Each year at Christmas, my brother and I anticipated finding a Brooks Brothers shirt under the tree, a tastefully boxed broadcloth button-down, either white or a soft workaday blue the color of waves in Winslow Homer's Caribbean. He succeeded in passing to his sister's children a love of the arts, especially my sister Treva and me. When she was eight, he awarded her a Brownie box camera and taught her to shoot and develop film. Somehow my brother Doug, the youngest among us, was less susceptible, being of a more practical bent, though it's true that he jokingly confessed that he was seeking to master "the manly art" of needlepoint.

My uncle supplemented his love of figure drawing with a passion for photography, setting up a complete studio in the basement to develop film, using chemicals that most amateurs eschewed. As a result, our lives from infants to febrile teenagers were documented, mostly in black and white. Because he worked in the paper's art department, several times he directed photographers to shoot us for the paper's Sunday magazine supplement. There is a cover shot of five or six of us as kids at Halloween, costumed and standing like jolly mendicants at the door of our neighbors, the Merckes. There we stand, an assembly of vagabonds, expectant with gaping paper bags and resembling the hopeful faces of displaced children in Europe, our contemporaries. Our mendicant band consisted of a pirate, a cowboy, a gypsy dancer, and my friend Robert Mercke got up in a skeleton suit. There is another of us—this one probably for filler—as young entrepreneurs, having set up a Kool-Aid stand, hawking tattered Superman comics and *Little LuLu, Two-Fisted Tales*, and *Tales from the*

Crypt as well as discarded toys along the curbside under the shade of the Merckes' two large maples—a local read on the genre scenes of vintage Norman Rockwell. Art is imitation, Plato tells us, and, I would add, inventive divergence. When Uncle Louis gave my sister that box Kodak, he hoped his hobby would take hold in her. He must have recognized implicitly that I lacked the patience and ability to follow directions that snapping and developing pictures required.

For me it was words. When I came in late on weekends to find him in his armchair reading, he would quiz me about the meaning of certain words, referring me to his oversized *Oxford English Dictionary* on a shelf to one side of the mantel. He encouraged me to maintain a word list, and soon I had the habit of looking up strange words I came across, using and misusing them on my parents and friends. In college as an English major my inflated raft of words was to founder on the shore of Freshman English.

My instructor in English 101, a gravelly ex-Navy man from Boston who once threw an eraser at a boneheaded student, was a stickler for logic and organization, a champion of the well-crafted thesis. He had little patience with the use of big words when modest ones would do. He pointed out that the polysyllabic word found only in a dictionary was not always the right word, and in fact, was *rarely* the right word. The right word, in his view, was the best word, the word that transferred meaning, big or small—*le mot juste* as the Frenchman Flaubert a little pretentiously put it. In my first papers this instructor scolded me for using inflated diction, making his point by downgrading me and desecrating my prose with hash marks. It was a lesson I learned only painfully and of which I am still a student.

Uncle Louis also fostered my love of history. Though my father told stories and had a keen interest in Kentucky's past, Uncle Louis awarded me a subscription to the Landmark Series of books published by Random House for young readers. Soon I was addicted. Each month a hardbound book with a colorful jacket and comfortably readable type would appear in the mail—Grant and Lee, the Erie Canal, Thomas Edison, the Alamo, and dozens of others. I devoured them all and have recently collected a set for my grandson in hopes that he too will catch the bug. Uncle Louis also encouraged my writing and did not frown, as my father did, when I announced that I proposed to major in English. Though my father too was a servant of words, he made his living by applying the language of the law in very precise and sometimes artful ways before a jury. The difference was that his language always rested on a bedrock of horse sense and unambiguous practicality. Subtlety and imagination were not for him either as a goal or even a desirable possibility. Myself I saw as a Hemingway or want-to-be poet, having adventures and plucking keys on a battered Underwood. But it was primarily from my uncle that I derived a love of words and the ways language can be teased to work, especially in the mysterious, uncertain, and hazy uplands of metaphor.

Finally, Uncle Louis is responsible as much as anyone for my love of art and my efforts to create it. Fascinated by the violence of war as a child, I drew stick figures in ranked formations on imaginary battlefields. Later, I took an art course or two as an undergraduate, one of them painting. In middle age, I started doing watercolor landscapes and joined a figure-drawing class, working with walnut ink a friend had taught me to make. In my late sixties, I had an impulse to teach myself to draw, learning again through imitation. I would start each morning with sketches in the journals I have kept since 1984, usually basing what I draw on images from the masters. Starting with Michelangelo, Da Vinci, and Albrecht Durer, I jumped past Antoine Watteau ahead to the Impressionists, especially Degas whose ballerinas, racehorses, and bathing nudes have been an inspiration. From Degas it was an easy step to Cézanne and Van Gogh's notebooks and then to Käthe Kollwitz and other twentieth-century masters. Only recently did it occur to me that I derive this love of drawing from sessions in the living room as a child when Uncle Louis's pencil would scratch on paper, revealing images that captured the lineaments of what was before him, usually a head or a torso caught in his unerring eye. So in addition to the image embodied in language I owe him a love of line and shadow on paper, hundreds of them accumulating over more than a decade.

Religion? Uncle Louis was a lapsed Catholic in a family of lapsed German Catholics (his sister and probably his parents, my maternal grandparents). He was an apostate monk in the comfortable cell of his armchair. I never knew him to enter a church except perhaps through his imagination or illustrations in an art book to see the Sistine Chapel. He was what people on the right today describe disparagingly as a secular humanist, as many churchgoers I know are at root. His head was locked into the foundational Greek philosophers, and their world of Socratic dialogue and Stoicism must have been an evening comfort to him.

Though he had friends, Louis Dey was not, at least when I knew him, a nightlifer. Yes, he went out to parties occasionally though I never knew him to date. Not gay, he had—I somehow learned—a woman in his heart, a married woman for whom he carried a torch until old age finally snuffed out the flame. A closet alcoholic in his elder years, his preferred beverage was Dewar's White Label Scotch unchastened by water though he also partook, ironically, of Christian Brothers wine.

For company he owned a pet, a spoiled spitz named Filbert that my sister remembers as crazy. One of his eyes had a black ring around it, giving him a pugnacious and off-kilter look. Outside, Filbert had the habit of barking at nothing, leaping and making little acrobatic circuits in the air, intimidating the neighbors' German Shepherd, Pickles, who, when passing our house, would cross the street to escape with impunity and then recross at the next door neighbors' and resume his walk. Often Filbert would snap at us, as sometimes he would his indulgent master. With his privileged status came a strain of canine perverseness. Outside, he would always bark at passersby and run erratic orbits in the yard. Inside, he had a trick of running circuits in the house, from the kitchen to the dining room, to the living room, and to the hallway back to the kitchen. It was the only predictable thing about him. He would run in only one direction, and sometimes—out of a perverse sense of humor or cruelty or a combination of both—we would close a swinging door between the kitchen and dining room, causing collisions. That flummoxed him. Like his master, Filbert till the end of his days was nothing if he was not predictably, self-definingly himself.

Unlike my father, a taciturn man who kept his own counsel, Uncle Louis loved to talk, and from him I derived first an appreciation of the give-and-take of conversation and verbal sparring. Add the voice of my sister Treva and the dinner table became an arena in which each participant had to defend his or her views. Neither my sister nor I were bashful about expressing our opinions, a habit of mind that grew from table debates. My father, laconic in the tradition of the Stoics, mainly listened. Occasionally, he would step in to correct or temper what he regarded to be views that were "out there." Though I'm sure he had his ideas, his primary world was the professional one of depositions and trials, his lodestone what the hypothetical reasonable man would do or think in given circumstances. Abstractions were avoided in his world of solid surfaces, a world of determinable cause, effects, and legal consequences. His opinions were largely conventional and rooted in what he described as the "real" world. No matter how abstruse the cloudy sky above him, he, like Thoreau, always kept one hand on the huckleberry bush. He had little use for what he regarded as "courthouse talk," especially about such subjects as the arts or social issues. By nature conservative, he was a registered Democrat but evolved into a closet Republican, distrustful of President Johnson's war on poverty and the "Greeaaat Society," which he usually described in a dismissive tone. His views were time-tried inheritances from the rural setting of his youth. He valued action that produced tangible results whether he was clearing a fencerow or defending his client from liability for failure to yield a right of way. Uncle Louis, contrariwise, must have somewhere encountered the dialogues of Plato and often went into a mode of successive questions, ever reducing my ill-thought answers to still more questions, often to extremes of absurdity and pea-splitting.

Uncle Louis and my father lived in different worlds, having only two things in common. They both loved my mother. They both loved gardening, though Uncle Louis was strictly flowers, my father vegetables and fruits as well as his own superabundance of flowers, his old-age recreation. If my father had his feet soldered to the ground, Uncle Louis brandished artistic flair. I learned recently that his celebrated banner for the paper had two e's in different type faces, which would have been anathema to typesetters of the day. For him, life was a constant flow of words as natural as water. And as limpid. Though they had their differences, one winter my father brought Uncle Louis a large load of manure for his flower beds as a Christmas gift. The recipient was too grateful to see any irony in the gift.

My brother recalls Uncle Louis teaching him what a pun was by saying something he picked up from Vaudeville: "Bread, bread, the actor said, and the curtain came down with a roll." His insistence on an aesthetic of appealing visibility and clarity caused me for the first time to consider language seriously as an instrument of discovery and a means to construct a world on paper, an alternate reality. For sport as much as instruction, he sprang big words on me, persuading me that language was muscle, that one's worth was measured largely by an ability to clothe and articulate thought.

Uncle Louis made his way through life until his drinking and sedentary lifestyle caught up with him in the form of a stroke. Retiring "a master of the graphic arts," as one associate described him in 1969, he died October

9, 1973. A witness to our growing up, he genuinely loved his niece and nephews. Books, the visual arts, drawing, a flair for language, Broadway plays, and Brooks Brothers—Uncle Louis gave me what no one had given him. In addition to his prized pyramidal hornbeams, he planted trees in whose shade he knew he would never sit.

POEM FOR MY FATHER

Days after his death
we found the faith he left us
in the shed:

six late tomatoes
shining on the sill,
stems carefully plucked,
green skins to the sun,

the last of his garden
surviving frost
to ripen in our blood.

EPILOGUE

Somewhere I ran across a statement, supposedly made by Thomas Jefferson, that he was a farmer so that his son could be a lawyer so that his son could be a poet. Those words caught my eye because they mirrored the generational progression (some would say regression) in my own family. When I tried to verify the source, I found a similar sentiment in a letter John Adams sent to his wife on May 12, 1780:

> I must study Politicks and War that my sons have liberty to study Mathematicks and Philosophy. My sons ought to study Mathematicks and Philosophy, Geography, natural History, Naval Architecture, in order to give their children a right to study Painting, Poetry, Musick, Architecture, Statuary, Tapestry and Porcelaine.

Whatever the source, whatever the precise wording, the essential idea is that fathers labor or revolutionize to better prospects for their sons and daughters. Implicit is the Enlightenment notion of self-improvement with a bias toward the ascendancy of the arts as well as inherent optimism about the future. This is the American ideal of generational progress that replaced, at least in theory, the endless repetition of cycles in which most of the world was frozen during much of Western history, a condition in which class dictated destiny with little hope for change in economic prospects or the pursuit of happiness over the generations. This explains why, as I learned, Reuben Taylor, as a young farmer struggled so hard to put his sons in school and why he accepted a loan or gift from his brother to educate them. It also explains why my own father, though often skeptical, never flinched or complained about his sons and daughter going to graduate school though such opportunities required sacrifices.

If we reflect at all on our origins, we necessarily become students of our ancestors. Where did we come from? How did we get here? What qualities in our parents shaped who we are as adults? What effect have we had on our own children? Such study is full of revelations large and small, serendipitous and sometimes grave and painful. Genealogical resources have made the process accessible to virtually everyone with a cursor and a little curiosity.

Like the archaeologist with her sieve, we never know what will be unearthed, memories buried haphazardly in the great midden of our individual pasts. A few years ago I attended the auction of a sizable library that I—a sometime bookseller—had once appraised in Frankfort. It was held in a rural auction barn I'd never visited, and I arrived after bidding had started. Moving among the long tables, my eyes flitted along the upturned spines, some familiar, some new to me, finding little to perk my interest. Then I spotted a stack of what appeared to be paperbound yearbooks with "Kentucky Military Institute 1925–1926" on the cover and another with "1927–1928" in the same bold no-nonsense typeface. "Damn," I said to myself, knowing that my father had graduated from K.M.I. in 1924. I had missed him by a year. Yearbooks, of course, have pictures featuring the senior class, but he had graduated a year earlier than the earlier of the two. Curious and guardedly hopeful, I bought them anyway. When I fetched them home, I first opened the later one. There were team pictures, promotional photos of the school, its faculty, a message from the commandant as well as a printed roster of cadets. No images of my father. Disappointed, I opened the earlier one and almost immediately found a class picture of fifteen or twenty uniformed young men looking martial and confident.

And there, unmistakably, was my father, probably eighteen, standing on the front row among a rising tier of his classmates. Wearing jodhpurs and high boots, a pleated tunic, a dark tie, he was costumed like a storm trooper in training, still relatively innocent. It was the earliest photo I had ever seen of him, a wonder. The earliest I had previously seen was a snapshot of him in a swimsuit in the early thirties, looking pale, slight, and almost scrawny among a group of friends that included a girlish version of my mother, by then probably his fiancée. There were no surviving photos of him in childhood, none in his early teens. Kodaks had not yet widely circulated among the American middle class that was soon to start documenting itself with great ardor. Thumbing the pages, I found another, this one of the 1923–24 football team in which he is wearing a heavy white sweater with a bold K on the chest. And another with the basketball team in which he looks every bit the teenager he was. I made copies of these glossy photos and shared them with my brother and sister, who shared them with their children. What difference did all of this make? A blank portion of his life had come alive to me. My mother had told me he had lettered in four sports, one of them wrestling, which he continued in college. To me, this physical glimpse into his past meant everything, another small gap filled, another stitch of identity sewn.

Where there were no photos, each recollection became a snapshot that contributed to understanding the larger mystery of my father's, or anyone's, life. Some evidence was direct and retrievable, as in the memory of the pedigree English Pointers that he ordered when I was nine or ten—Tick and Beau. They came in crates as pups by train from a breeder somewhere in Canada. Though I never heard about it, my mother must have complained about this extravagance. She would definitely have put her foot down had there been any effort to bring them home as pets. When they arrived, I can remember going to fetch them at the Louisville and Nashville Railroad Station at 9th and Broadway in downtown Louisville. The dogs were brothers—noble-headed, short haired with flecks and blotches of reddish brown on their sides and backs, and my father wanted the pleasure of grooming and training them as hunters in the field. There is a framed photo of him bending over Tick in a slanting field somewhere, his hand on his back as if to steady him, obviously posed in training. From the outset it was clear they couldn't live in the city, so Cousin Lucy was persuaded to give them a home in the country. There they grew half-wild, roaming and eventually running with other dogs in a pack. Soon it was obvious that they, left largely on their own outside, were too much for Lucy and Mony.

Training Tick.

One was severely injured by getting entangled in a barbed wire fence. Both continued to run with a pack of dogs and came to no good end. For my father they must have represented the self he dreamed of being—a bird hunter of quail and doves and ducks—the self he became too busy and too long in the tooth to be. Most of his hunting must have been confined to elusive birds in imaginary fields just as his collection of hunting and fishing books permitted him to experience vicariously what he could no longer personally enact. Similarly, though he also loved to fish and took me with him on fishing expeditions as a child, that pastoral dream also languished in the press of life increasingly full and often anxious, sometimes frenetic. At the end of his life, he had not been fishing for decades. He and my Uncle Lawrence (whose first name became my middle name) had secreted a cache of lures and flies strung on multiple lines from the rafters of Lawrence's attic, which had been converted to a tackle shop, a sportsman's hoard that neither had used for years—each hoping to step into that parallel life at some indeterminate moment of fulfillment. Lawrence was a banker, and I suspect he regarded fishing equipment as a kind of savings account from which they both could draw nostalgic dividends.

In addition to parallel lives, such deferred gratification took another form for my father, one that was more idealistic but in fact was more gestured and symbolic than a realistic possibility. For years he paid membership dues for himself and his two sons because the Jefferson County Sportsmen's Club sponsored an annual quail release. Each member was allotted a certain number of boxed quail to set loose in the wild. A savvy hunter would stock a certain field with the prospect of replenishing depleted flocks and thus eventually restore good hunting. We would go along to a designated pickup place and collect our quail, and my father would surreptitiously take them to undisclosed locations for release—I suspect around Worthington—because he believed in the project, yes, but also with the subliminal hope of taking up his prized Parker shotgun to hunt. It occurs to me now that it was a kind of aspirational exercise that gave him satisfaction, sustaining a remnant of the hunting cult of his youth that kept him in the game without guilt since it benefited wildlife whose habitats were shrinking in the face of development and urban sprawl.

How my father regarded me I won't try to answer. As I ponder the question, I suddenly remember a winter ice skating party when he conducted six or seven of us to a farm pond near Worthington. I was maybe thirteen. Each of us had been provided with an old-fashioned pair of ice skates, high-topped with tight-laced leather and a single blade running along the soles. The farm pond belonging to one of his farmer friends covered the space of maybe two tobacco barns. After we'd laced up our skates, he gave us an admonition: "See that spot across the pond?"

We gazed out over the gray glazed surface and saw a dark spot with what appeared to be a bubble underneath.

"Don't go near that spot," he warned us, "or you'll fall in. The ice is too thin."

Soon we were swerving in circles about the pond, and I, testing limits, drew near the shallow end we'd been warned to avoid. Too late I realized my skates had carried me too close, and sure enough I found myself waist deep in freezing water. Which meant all of us had to go home. "I told you," my father said, "not to go near that end, and what did you do? Went right to it," answering his own question. The others reluctantly returned to the banks, unlaced their skates, and piled into the jeep, my older sister especially miffed at me for spoiling the outing. "Didn't I tell you?" my father said, as the punishing cold worked its way through my wet clothes and into memory to resurface almost a lifetime later. An artist friend titled one of his paintings of a wigged-out teenager as *the awkward years*, and those years must have also been a test of restraint and forbearance for my parents as they witnessed sinews, hormones, and pure silliness flex and blunder toward a steadier path.

That steadier path, I suppose, gradually was gained, most of it after his death in 1974 when I completed my second graduate English degree, found a job teaching, married, bought an old house and a mortgage, helped start a book business, and proceeded to have children—three of them— and to write and publish as part of my own parallel life. I was reminded of how Zorba the Greek from Niko Kazantzakis's great novel of that name responded to the naive and impressionable young Englishman, his employer, who asked if he was married. The quote was something like, "Yes, boss—wife, job, kids, house, mortgage—the whole catastrophe." Well, the whole catastrophe is what answers for a life, one which is inextricably tied to my father's more than biologically, but through every attitude, outlook, and mannerism of speech and habit that I inherited from him—too close to it then to recognize the watermarks, his imprint, on the person I became—for better or worse. Now and probably then,

I am never far from the khakied figure standing by his getaway jeep, his friend and his rearing hunt dog caught in a moment of contentment, an expression of perplexed euphoria playing across his face.

Putting the pond of memory aside, sometimes my discoveries turned from the past and took aim at the future and the continuity of generations. In the early spring of 2020 my son Willis and his wife Lucy, expecting their first child, were able to leave Manhattan where they live and practice law, wisely departing a month or so before the COVID-19 pandemic accelerated in high gear. They returned to Kentucky, at least temporarily, where on April 19, 2020, Lucy gave birth to a healthy son, Philip Reuben Taylor. Fathers beget fathers. Fathers, sons.

— END —

ACKNOWLEDGMENTS

I am grateful to the following publications for printing earlier versions of some of these essays.

An earlier version of "Crescent Hill" appeared in *Place Gives Rise to Spirit: Writers on Louisville*, Kathleen Driskell, Editor, Fleur-de-Lis Press, Louisville, 2001. "A Wet Christmas" was previously published in *Kentucky's Twelve Days of Christmas*, edited by James B. Goode, *Kentucky Monthly*, Frankfort, 2012. An earlier version of "Guineas and Griddle Cakes: Two Kentucky Portraits," was printed in *Savory Memories*, L. Elisabeth Beattie, Editor, University Press of Kentucky, Lexington, 1998. An earlier version of "My Civil War Education" was published in *Kentucky Humanities, A State Divided: The Civil War in Kentucky*, Kentucky Humanities Council, Lexington, 2013. A version of the introduction was published as "My Father" in *From Pen to Page II, More Writings from the Bluegrass Writers Coalition* (2023). "Mistletoe" was previously published in *A Kentucky Christmas*, edited by George Ella Lyon, University Press of Kentucky, Lexington, 2003. Thanks to Gray Zeitz for providing a key photo of David Orr and to graphic master Gene Burch for his invaluable assistance and suggestions on design. I am most grateful to Katerina Stoykova, my publisher and longtime friend whose good sense and efficiency kept me on course. I owe special thanks to my son Willis for his efforts in researching sources for "In the Matter of Reuben" and for his meticulous editing of the manuscript, improving it wherever he put his hand. And to my daughter Julia for her unfailing technical assistance in preparing the manuscript, and to my sister, Treva, and brother, Douglas for sharing their recollections, many of which I lifted red-handed into the text.

ABOUT THE AUTHOR

Richard Taylor is the author of numerous collections of poetry, two historical novels, and several books relating to Kentucky history, including *Elkhorn: Evolution of a Kentucky Landmark*. A former Kentucky poet laureate, he has received two creative writing fellowships from the National Endowment for the Arts as well as an Al Smith Award from the Kentucky Arts Council. Educated at the University of Kentucky (bachelor's and Ph.D. in English), he also holds a master's degree (English) and a J.D. from the University of Louisville. Practicing law for a few months, he gave up legal practice, a leave-taking he regards as his gift to the Commonwealth of Kentucky. During graduate school he taught in high schools across Kentucky with the Poetry-in-the-Schools Program through the Kentucky Arts Council, editing an anthology of student writing called *Cloud Bumping*. Embarking on a career in education, he taught at Kentucky State University in Frankfort until retiring in 2008. During that time he taught in the Governor's School for the Arts as well as serving as director of the Governor's Scholars Program on two campuses. He also spent a year in Denmark as a scholar-teacher in the Fulbright Program, also teaching a graduate course at Kangwon University in Korea as well as short periods teaching abroad in England and Ireland in a studies-abroad program. He has received publication awards from the Kentucky Historical Society and the Thomas C. Clark Medallion for his Elkhorn book as well as receiving a Distinguished Professor Award at KSU. Recently retired after fourteen years from Transylvania University as Keenan Visiting Writer, he was inducted into the Kentucky Writers Hall of Fame. He is co-owner of Poor Richard's Books and lives on a small farm outside Frankfort, Kentucky.